The Paradox of Pain

Historical and psychological sources informing this book include works by Alison Des Forges, Scott Straus, Phil Clark, Roméo Dallaire, Judith Butler, Idith Zertal, Tom Segev, Ilan Pappé, Edward Said, Judith Butler, Bessel van der Kolk, Roméo Dallaire, David Rieff, UNICEF, Human Rights Watch, Save the Children, and Human Rights Watch, among others. Full citations are provided in Appendix II.

Scripture quotations, where cited, are taken from the *Holy Bible, New International Version (NIV)* unless otherwise noted.

Published by Jama Tales Press
Houston, Texas

ISBN: 979-8-9934588-6-1 – paperback
ISBN: 979-8-9934588-7-8 – hard cover
For permission requests, contact:
contact@jamatales.com
www.jamatales.com

THE PARADOX OF PAIN

By Mariela G. George

Dedication and Gratitude

The idea for this book has been lingering in me for a very long time,
but its title and meaning took clear shape
after a sermon by Pastor Sang
at New Life Church, Houston, Texas.

I still remember that day —
the silence between the words,
when something sacred stirred within me
and I finally understood:
pain is not punishment.
It is God's invitation to return home.

I did not know it then,
but the Holy Spirit had already begun His work —
whispering through the cracks in my soul,
shaping this story long before I could name it.

Also, to Lisa and Pastor Eric,
thank you for your patience,
for seeing me when I was hidden,
for opening your hearts,
and for leading me, step by trembling step,
through Jesus —
into peace, into safety, into light.

And this book…
this book is also my prayer —
for my sons Viktor and Aleks,
for my mother,
for my cousins, Ralitsa and Kalin,
for Yen, Kelly, and Elizabeth,
and for my grandchildren — current and future.

May God keep them in His gentle palms,
soothe their pain,
guide them through every storm,
and open their hearts
to the beauty of this world —
the kind that can never be fully seen
or felt
without Him.

**To all who have ever asked "Why pain?" —
may these pages remind you
that every wound can become a doorway
if you let God walk you through it.**

Author's Note

My life was a rollercoaster. A constant collision between what I believed, what I endured, and what refused to remain silent inside me.

Until recently, I was convinced understanding was the same as knowing, and knowing was enough. I collected ideas. I analyzed suffering. I explained pain. I learned how to survive — and mistook survival for wisdom. If you are holding this book, there is a chance you recognize that distinction too.

This is not a book about pain from a safe distance. I am not an observer. It is written from the depths of my abyss — from grief that could not be reasoned away, from questions that refused polite answers, from moments when faith felt less like comfort and more like risk. I did not come to the conclusions in these pages easily. I came to them reluctantly, often resisting them, sometimes offended by them, and frequently broken by what they required of me.

You will not find simple reassurance here. But you will find honesty.

I am not interested in "defending" God by explaining Him away, nor in accusing Him of the world's suffering. I am interested in truth — the kind that can bear weight, endure scrutiny, and still stand when comfort fails. The kind that does not collapse under grief, injustice, or silence.

If at times my words sound firm, it is not because I have never doubted. It is because I have. If they sound uncompromising, it is not because I lack compassion, but because I have learned what happens when truth is endlessly softened to spare our feelings — it eventually abandons us when we need it most.

This book asks difficult questions, some of which may feel familiar, others unsettling. It does not attempt to answer all of them equally, nor does it pretend neutrality where none exists. My perspective is shaped by Scripture, by lived experience, and by the conviction that love and truth are not opposites — and that separating them is one of the deepest wounds of our time.

You do not need to agree with me to read this book. You do not even need to believe. But I ask one thing of you: do not read defensively. Read as someone willing to be encountered — not by an argument, but by a reality that may name things you have felt but never articulated.

There will be moments here that challenge cherished assumptions. Others may reopen wounds you thought were sealed. If that happens, pause. You are not being rushed. This book does not demand speed, only honesty.

I poured my soul on those pages not to teach you, but to share my testimony with you — how I learned, slowly and painfully, that pain does not disappear when ignored, that meaning cannot be manufactured, and that God is not most fully revealed in our certainty, but in what remains when certainty collapses.

This is a book about suffering, but it is not written in despair. It is written in hope — not the fragile hope of optimism, but the costly hope that emerges when illusions fall away and something truer remains.

If you are looking for permission to avoid pain, this book will disappoint you. If you are looking for language to understand it, to endure it, and perhaps — eventually — to be transformed by it, then you are welcome here.

Take your time.
Read slowly.
And know this: whatever questions you bring, you are not the first to ask them — and you are not alone in your quest.

Mariela G. George

"… your kingdom will be restored to you when you acknowledge that Heaven rules."
Daniel 4:26

"For by grace you have been saved."
Ephesians 2:8

THE SENTENCE

Written in college. I did not know then that I was describing my own awakening.

One, two, three… once again! Come on!
Nothing. Nothing happens.
I am painfully straining to do something so simple — to open my eyes.
But I cannot.
The eyelids remain heavy, refusing to yield to effort.

I feel the violent pressure beneath them — my eyeballs furiously rotating, jumping, striking against the walls of their orbits like prisoners desperate to escape.
They search for a way out of the dark cave that holds them captive.
The growing grayness is unbearable.

Long ago…
My eyes were familiar with color; they remembered motion, the caress of air, the simple beauty of outlines.
They had known prayer and fairness, hope and fragile faith.
They had glowed with happiness, flashed with the ice crystals of hate, burned with the lava of passion, and dimmed with the low embers of agony.
They had wept deep rivers of tears and endured the desert thirst of pain.

They were human — absolutely human — my eyes.

And they refused to accept the gray-white illusion of clouds, that insipid charity of light flickering outside.
It was too unreal.
Yet, in truth, it was their only reality now.

My eyes…
My eyes craved horizons — sunrises and sunsets, distances and mysteries, vastness and the unapproachable unknown.
They longed for seas and skies.
But the eyelids, with unexpected cruelty, pressed down again.

One, two, three… last effort! A way out!

Suddenly, space erupts from the darkness — flooding my essence with the fierce rush of perspective, intensity, and discovery — obscure, unexplored, unsuspected.

There are no outlines.

There are no horizons.

No roads.

On the other side, there is only an inexplicable vastness, swirling sensations, and irresistible magnetism.

Power.

It vibrates around me, touches me with cautious fingers, binds me with fine electric threads, and slowly — gently — pulls me inward.

Inward, toward the one inevitable alternative.

My pupils widen in astonishment.

...Warm dampness blankets me.

Tender darkness. Softness. Silence that venerates.

Only tup-tup, tup-tup — the heart measures the moments of an inner beginning.

Beautiful. Calm. Real.

Then — a sudden convulsion.

An unseen push.

Unrealized, tasteless pain.

The first gulp of air tears through my lungs, vibrating with oxygen atoms in my blood, filling me, becoming my nature.

Pain.

The one true proof of my existence now, the beginning of my being, the memory of Before.

Then, with the force of a tornado, the shadows rush in:

Bare cliffs and unfathomable depths.

Burned fields and twisted lips sinking in the mud.

A raped white moon —

At the very edge of the pier,

in the only city of three lakes[1].

---

1. Burgas, a city in Bulgaria where I was born

Directions had lost their roads, and roads had lost their directions.
Never-kissed lips, and kisses that never found lips.

Phantoms.

Born of darkness, roaming aimlessly, balancing upon the thin thread of hope.
Phantoms, the moonwalkers of a moonless world.
One, two, three…
I make one last effort before losing my mind to this terrible, indescribable world within me.
My eyes are thirsty for light.
My eyes cannot surrender.
One more try!
They want to know the purpose.
Once again!
To understand the meaning.
One more effort!
To find the cause.
My eyes continue their painful, weary descent into the depths of my being — into the nucleus of my own womb — seeking to reclaim their power, to lift those merciless eyelids that guard the passage to Genesis.
My eyes — tired, wounded, covered with sores, my human, deeply human eyes — are charged with light, with boundless scope.
But they are weak — so weak — my eyes.
And to lift those merciless eyelids, they must endure the pain of surrender.

Author's Reflection – When I Finally Understood What I Had Written

I wrote *"The Sentence"* a lifetime ago — still in college, still learning what it meant to be human. At the time, I thought it was simply a strange, emotional story about pain and awakening.
Now I know that it was my soul writing before my mind could understand.

I see it now — God had already begun His work in me. He was shaping my spirit long before I could name His presence. He would not let me give up on myself, even when I no longer knew how to hold on.

For years, I kept searching for that "Power" I felt inside — something that could lift me above despair, something that could make sense of suffering. I searched through philosophies, through people, through silence. And only now do I realize:
the Power I was seeking was God Himself —
the One who never left,
who refused to surrender my soul to darkness,
who transformed every scar into a doorway back to Him.

What I wrote as a college student was the cry of a heart that didn't yet know who it was crying to. What I write now is the answer — whispered back through time by the same God who had already heard me then.

Through His Eyes

Lyrics by Mariela G. George

"I was the prodigal drowning in vain,
A dog returning to the same old chains.
But He tore the night with a bleeding crown,
Pulled me up when the world dragged me down.
He took my rage, turned it into light,
Gave me the will to stand and fight.
I'm more than the war that carved my skin,
I'm the soul He refused to give in."
(Find the Album of songs in Appendix II)

PROLOGUE

Before the Word

Have you ever felt so overwhelmed by life that you wished you could erase everything and start again?

You stare into the void, trying to remember where you lost yourself, where time slipped away. There is a loud, unsettling noise in your ears — and yet, inside your chest, a deep and terrifying silence. You lift your fingers to your neck, searching for your pulse, just as you were taught long ago. Or was it yesterday? Your fingers tremble. The pulse eludes you. Your breath feels trapped inside your lungs, unable to find a way out.

The pain in your chest — sharp, burning — arrives as a warning. Somewhere beneath the panic, an old instinct stirs — carbon dioxide must leave to make room for oxygen.

Exhale.

Inhale.

The simplest act now feels impossible.

Darkness settles in.

There is something about darkness I have always feared — the loneliness of it, the inability to see, the creeping presence of the Unknown. Fear does not always announce itself with noise. Sometimes it arrives quietly. It stills the body. It teaches the heart to hide. When true fear takes hold, everything becomes an enemy — sound, movement, even breath.

I lived like this for much of my life: frozen in the dark.

Eventually, I learned how to move. I transformed fear into motion — determination, urgency, momentum. Any direction was better than stillness. "If you're going through hell, keep moving," I told myself. And I moved. Fast. Cities. Countries. Jobs. Relationships. I mistook movement for life, endurance for wisdom.

Running is easier than seeing.

When you run, there is no time to ask where you are going.

So, I kept running — even when I was exhausted — because stopping felt dangerous. Every runner knows the worst thing to do is stop. And while I ran, my life quietly passed me by.

When everything finally collapsed — the structures I had built, the certainties I trusted, the life I believed I was holding together — I thought I had lost everything. But loss has a way of asking better questions than success ever does.

We are all given a story. It has a past, a present, and a future — at least as we understand time. But fear binds us to what was and pulls us toward what has not yet come, tightening like a rope around the present moment until we can no longer move freely at all.

Fear does not disappear. It never truly leaves. But when it is faced — not outrun — it weakens. And to face it requires something far more difficult than speed. It requires presence. And presence requires letting go.

But how do you release the past without losing yourself? How do you stop living ahead of your life without erasing your story?

I did not know the answers when I entered the darkness. I only knew that I could no longer run. I had reached the place where movement stopped working, where endurance failed, where silence demanded to be answered.

And it was there — before explanations, before certainty, before meaning — that I encountered the Word.

"In the beginning was the Word, and the Word was with God, and the Word was God." — John 1:1

This story does not begin with understanding. It begins with surrender.

And it does not end in isolation.

All journeys worth taking are meant to be shared.

CHAPTER 1

The Salt of the Earth

Many times, life strikes us with cruelty — unexpected, overwhelming, burning deep into the soul. It shakes the ground beneath us. Sometimes it is so intense that it dries the tears in our eyes and leaves behind a heavy, unbearable emptiness in the chest.

When this happens, we feel attacked.

And so, we move into defense mode — because this is what our culture and our science have taught us is the natural human response: fight, flight, or freeze. We are trained to avoid the "freeze" response, because the other two feel more active, more powerful, more aligned with survival. When cruelty strikes, we feel compelled to either run or fight.

I am not speaking here about life-or-death situations. I am speaking about everyday relationships — work, friendship, family, intimacy. When cruelty enters these spaces, we are tempted to respond in kind: with explanations, arguments, sarcasm, and cleverness. We want to respond. We want to save face. We want to release the pressure in our chest and reclaim our dignity.

And we almost always find justification for doing so.

Sometimes we even manipulate the truth — subtly, convincingly — to fit a narrative where we remain in control, where we do not "give up," where we keep fighting. We tell ourselves that words exist for communication, and that if we do not speak, nothing can be resolved.

That is true.

But how we use truth matters just as much as whether it is true.

Silence is also communication. Sometimes it speaks louder than words ever could. I once believed that silence meant avoidance.

I was wrong.

Sometimes silence is not withdrawal from truth, but refusal of escalation. It is stepping out of anger. It is choosing to stop the vicious cycle of provocation. It is calming the ego and refusing to manipulate reality to feel powerful. It is handing the situation fully back to God.

Jesus Himself often remained silent when hearts were hardened.

When chosen, silence is not weakness. In a world full of noise, echoes, and mirrors demanding reactions, silence can say:

I will not fight for power.

I will not defend my ego.

I will not respond from the flesh.

Silence can be obedience. And obedience does not guarantee rescue — but it does guarantee God's faithfulness. Sometimes God delivers not by winning the battle for us, but by removing us from it altogether.

Occasionally, cruelty presents itself not as a pattern, a conflict, or a long unfolding struggle — but simply as an event.

Something that happens to us.

Or something we happen into.

Regardless, it arrives without warning — uninvited, unannounced, unexplainable. It strikes out of nowhere and leaves us breathless.

Empty.

There is no time to prepare, no space to reason, no language ready to receive it. One moment life moves forward, stitched together by routine and expectation — and the next, it is torn open.

Cruelty, in its most devastating form, does not argue with us. It does not negotiate. It does not even accuse.

It simply **is.**

And when cruelty takes the form of an event, silence is no longer a choice. It is imposed. There are no words to answer with, no defenses to raise, no explanations that could possibly make sense of what has just occurred. All the strategies we rely on in everyday conflicts — logic, justification, confrontation — collapse instantly.

This is the kind of cruelty that does not ask for a response.

But it demands surrender.

***

November 25, 2023.

I am sitting in front of my computer in a small apartment in Plovdiv, Bulgaria, talking to my son. I am giving my opinion on the gingerbread houses he and my daughter-in-law have built. I can still see the pictures — small edible artworks covered in marshmallows and Skittles. Warmth. Smiles. A quiet countdown.

Little houses glowing with light and decorations.

Expectation. Christmas is just around the corner.

So is the arrival of my granddaughter — Aniko.

***

November 26, 2023.
1:01 p.m. Houston time.
21:01 in Bulgaria.

I am in front of my computer again, this time watching a movie. The soft sound of Facebook Messenger draws my attention to the right side of the screen.

"Two weeks ago, we had a full checkup."

The message is from my son, updating me on my daughter-in-law and my grandbaby. I smile and send a heart.

"Genetics, labs, CT, imaging — everything is fine."

I send another heart.

Before I can type a response, the messages keep coming.

"Today,
Aniko
is dead."

I will never be able to describe the abyss that cracked open in my chest.

The searing pain.

The tightening in my throat.

The weight.

The fear.

The harrowing scream of silence.

Even now, as I write these words, tears fall down my face — salty and honest reminders of what pain tastes like.

***

There are many ways to produce the salt we take for granted today — tiny white crystals we scarcely notice. In Jesus's time, salt was worth its weight in silver: a sacred symbol of endurance, preservation, and covenant.

It seasoned bread.

It cleansed wounds.

It sealed promises.

It marked holy offerings brought before the Lord.

To live without salt was to live without preservation — without protection from rot and ruin.

"You are the salt of the earth..." *(Matthew 5:13)*

Why would Jesus compare us to a substance that stings and heals, preserves and purifies — something so small, yet powerful enough to hold decay at bay?

I believe He was revealing not our importance, but our calling.

To preserve what is holy in a decaying world.

To carry healing into what festers.

To flavor despair with the taste of hope.

But to become salt, one must first be broken — just the natural order of formation.

In the depths of the seas — where chaos meets order — salt begins to form when water surrenders. When tides pull back. When movement gives way to stillness under the sun.

Rocks weather. Minerals dissolve. Pressure reshapes the earth.

And then evaporation begins — water, stripped away by heat, leaves behind what it always carried — hidden, essential, prevailing.

To become salt, water must endure fire from above. It must let go of what it was — fluid, restless, vast — and allow itself to be reduced, refined, concentrated. Only then does it reveal its purpose.

Salt is formed through loss.

Through pressure.

Through exposure.

Through time.

Isn't this the very process of sanctification?

***

There is salt in every tear we cry — the chemistry of grief, the evidence of love. Tears are how the soul releases what words cannot carry.

The same salt.

The same flow.

A different purpose.

Tears of sorrow and tears of joy come from the same place: surrender. When we weep, we release control. And in that release, we return to our truest state — dependent on the One who made us.

Perhaps the salt in our tears is the echo of that ancient calling: to preserve what matters, to heal what is broken, to remind the earth — and ourselves — that love is costly, but never wasted.

Salt preserves.

Pain transforms.

Tears testify.

And it is in brokenness that we begin to understand what Christ meant when He said:

"You are the salt of the earth."

CHAPTER 2

When Humanity Declares War on Pain

Long ago, I was asked what happiness is.

At the time, my answer came quickly and confidently: *the absence of pain.*

How little did I understand.

All our lives we strive to avoid pain — to minimize it, cure it, hide from it, run from it, eradicate it. And no matter how often we fail, we continue chasing the same illusion: a painless existence.

We make it our life's goal.

Our purpose.

The holy grail of our being.

And somewhere along the way, the line between good intentions and God's intentions disappears. We quietly assume yet another role — one that was never ours.

What happens when humanity declares war on pain?

History answers.

***

Between 1939 and 1941, behind the polished doors of Tiergartenstraße 4 in Berlin, a program was born whose name sounded like a bureaucratic code but would stain eternity: Action T4.

It began with forms.

With signatures.

With diagnoses.

Doctors — the very ones sworn to heal — were instructed to decide which lives were "worth living." Those deemed too fragile, too slow, too broken were marked for mercy deaths.

They called it euthanasia.

There was nothing merciful about it.

This was one of those moments in history when humanity made its war on pain explicit — and, in doing so, declared war on the image of God.

Action T4 was built on a single devastating lie: that suffering is meaningless, and therefore the sufferer is expendable.

The language was careful.

The paperwork precise.

The logic seductive: Remove pain. Restore purity. Relieve burden.

But every checkbox was a murder disguised as compassion.

This is what happens when a civilization erases its theology of suffering: Once the lie is accepted — that pain has no purpose — love itself becomes negotiable.

The cross is replaced by the scalpel.

The sanctity of life by the calculus of convenience.

Action T4 was not merely a policy. It was a revelation — of what the human heart becomes when it worships comfort instead of truth.

Every life deemed "unworthy" was a testimony interrupted. Every silenced breath was a question God placed in the world — and humanity refused to hear it.

The tragedy was not only in the deaths, but in the arrogance of believing we could heal the human condition by erasing its evidence.

Pain, in God's design, is never meaningless. It ties humanity to humility. It reminds us that we are neither gods nor experiments, but souls in need of grace.

***

The seventy thousand who were murdered during those years were not statistics.

"You are the salt of the earth..."

Ernst Lossa
Age: 14
"Diagnosis": "Asocial behavior"
Notes: Killed by lethal injection at Irsee psychiatric hospital in 1944.

Elfriede Lohse-Wächtler
Age: 39
Profession: Painter and graphic artist
Illness: Diagnosed with schizophrenia
Notes: Sterilized in 1935, murdered in 1940 at Pirna-Sonnenstein.

Gerhard Kretschmar
Age: Infant
Illness: Severe congenital disabilities
Notes: The first child killed under what became Action T4, after his parents petitioned Hitler directly for a "mercy death."

Mathilde Freudenberg
Age: 40
Profession: Homemaker
Illness: Depression after childbirth
Notes: Declared "incurably ill," transported, and killed despite being physically healthy.

Unknown child from Brandenburg
Age: 6
Illness: Speech delay
Notes: Recorded only as a transport number. No grave. No photograph.

....

....

The list continues...
Their names were erased from records, but...

"A book of remembrance was written before Him..."
The world called their deaths mercy.
Heaven called them witnesses.

***

When pain is declared meaningless, suffering becomes intolerable, and people —disposable. This is the logic that returns whenever comfort is sacred and endurance is perceived as offensive. Whenever dependency is seen as failure and weakness as defect.

But Scripture offers another word:

"Suffering produces perseverance; perseverance, character; and character, hope." (Romans 5:3-4)

Pain is not the enemy of meaning.

The refusal to bear it **is.**

***

Our tears leave behind evidence — that the heart still feels, still cares, still resists indifference.

Pain is not proof of God's absence. It is often the place where His work begins through preservation of the soul. And the real question is not why we suffer — but how long we will keep silencing what pain is exposing.

CHAPTER 3

I AM — When Truth Has a Name

"There are always two sides to every story."

I was taught this early in life. It sounded wise. Fair. Humane. It implied humility — the willingness to listen, to consider, to suspend judgment. And in many everyday matters, it carries a measure of truth. Human experience is complex. Memory is selective. Pain distorts perception. Two people can live through the same moment and carry away different wounds.

But somewhere along the way, this sentence quietly changed its meaning.

What began as an invitation to empathy became a denial of truth itself. Two perspectives became two truths. And truth, once anchored beyond us, began to drift — untethered, negotiable, endlessly revisable.

Scripture does not speak this way.

The God of the Bible does not introduce Himself as *one perspective among many.* He names Himself **I AM** — the unchanging center in a world that continually tries to relocate the center into the self. When truth loses its center, meaning fractures. Identity splinters. Language stretches until it can no longer carry weight. And confusion becomes the easiest doorway into control.

Yes, there are two memories. Two wounds. Two ways something felt. But truth is not a coin to be tossed between them. Truth is not negotiated. Truth simply *is.*

A world without a stable truth does not become free — it becomes fragile. There is an old Bulgarian story about Khan Kubrat. Near the end of his life, he called his sons to him and handed them a bundle of sticks. He asked them to break it. They tried — and failed. Bound together, the sticks would not yield. Then the Khan untied the bundle and handed them the sticks one by one.

Snap.

Snap.

Snap.

This wisdom appears across cultures for a reason. The human heart keeps rediscovering the same reality, even when it resists naming its source. Scripture does not whisper this truth; it declares it:

"A cord of three strands is not quickly broken." (Ecclesiastes 4:12)

"If one member suffers, all suffer together." (1 Corinthians 12:26)

Jesus Himself prayed for unity — not uniformity, not domination, but oneness rooted in love and truth:

"That all of them may be one, Father, just as you are in me and I am in you." (John 17:21)

And yet, we struggle to hold this. We remember unity most clearly when disaster strikes — when tragedy shatters our illusions of self-sufficiency. Then we need each other. Then we remember our shared humanity. But when life stabilizes, we return to separation. We divide, categorize, define, and defend. We build walls and call them identity. We imagine we are protecting ourselves, while slowly starving for peace.

Scripture explains why.

When humanity gathered at Babel, God did not judge diversity — He judged prideful consolidation. *"Let us make a name for ourselves,"* they said. It was not merely ambition. It was collective self-deification. Humanity was once again attempting to become its own center.

God's response was not destruction, but restraint.

The confusion of languages was not cruelty. It was mercy — a divine braking system before unity hardened into domination. Unrestrained unity under pride becomes a machine of destruction. History bears witness to this truth again and again.

And yet, God's story does not end at Babel.

At Pentecost[2], the Spirit descended — not to erase nations or languages, but to restore understanding under humility. Unity was reborn, not imposed. Difference remained, but confusion lost its power. This is the pattern of God's work: unity without erasure, plurality without fragmentation, truth without coercion.

---

2. Pentecost, has its origins in the Jewish festival of Shavuot (the Feast of Weeks), which celebrates the wheat harvest and the giving of the Law at Mount Sinai 50 days after Passover. It commemorates the descent of the Holy Spirit upon the Apostles and other followers of Jesus, an event often described as the "birthday of the Church" because it launched their public mission to the world. (Acts 2:1-47; Exodus 23:14–19; Leviticus 23:15–21; Deuteronomy 16:9–12; 1 Corinthians 16:8 and Acts 20:16)

So, the question is not whether unity or division is good.
The question is *what — or who — stands at the center.*
Truth does not belong to us. We belong to it.
And truth, in Scripture, has a Name.
"I AM WHO I AM." (Exodus 3:14)
And when truth has a center again, meaning can hold.

CHAPTER 4

When Truth Became Personal Property

Once truth lost its center, something else rushed in to replace it.

Our modern world has become a stage where we perform — role after role — crafting identities, curating narratives, hiding behind masks we invent. And when the spotlight fades, we kneel at a new altar, one that sounds compassionate but carries a heavy crown:

"Each person has their own truth — and it's valid."

At first glance, this language feels gentle. Protective. Humane. But beneath its softness lies a profound shift in authority. It does not merely defend people — it enthrones them. Truth becomes personal property. And once truth is owned, it can be weaponized.

I feel — therefore it is my reality, and I am justified.

You disagree — therefore you are dangerous.

I interpret — therefore I am the measure.[3]

A world like this cannot sustain unity, because unity requires a reference point higher than preference. When truth is severed from God, identity becomes something we must manufacture rather than receive. We define good instead of submitting to it. We rename what God has already named.

The result is not liberation.

It is weight.

Because if I must create myself, then I must also save myself. And the human soul was never designed to carry that kind of authority. Pride is not merely arrogance — it is an attempted promotion into godhood, followed by collapse.

I know this by experience.

In 2001, I graduated in Sociology from the University of Sofia. My thesis explored human sexuality as a social and cultural construct. I defended personal choice as the highest good. I treated identity as something societies invent and revise, as if human beings were merely projects of history.

---

3. Protagoras' famous dictum, "Man is the measure of all things" (homo mensura), posits that knowledge is subjective and relative to individual perception, meaning truth varies from person to person

I was educated.
I was articulate.
I was persuasive.
And I was blind.

My arguments sounded intelligent. They were academically praised. They opened doors for my career. And they also quietly opened a different door — to a place where nearly anything could be explained, reframed, or justified, if only the narrative was persuasive enough.

Looking back, I shudder at how a small fracture in truth can reshape an entire moral universe. What I called unbiased analysis was often human-centered reasoning with footnotes. I treated Scripture as a cultural artifact to be explained rather than a living revelation that judges cultures. I asked, "How this text can be interpreted by society?" instead of, "What does God demand of the human heart?"

Scripture warns us of this exact exchange

"Trust in the LORD with all your heart and lean not on your own understanding." (Proverbs 3:5)

"There is a way that seems right to a man, but its end is death." (Proverbs 14:12)

When truth becomes negotiable, pain becomes currency. Identity becomes armor. Movements form — often beginning with legitimate cries against injustice or suffering — but without a higher center, they harden. Pain is weaponized. Unity becomes coercive. Dissent is recast as violence. Not because division itself is evil but because pride survived the division. And unchecked division under pride becomes perpetual war.

And God is never indifferent.

The Flood was judgment by reset.

Babel was judgment by restraint.

When pride survives **restraint**, division hardens into hostility. What began as mercy became tribalism, rivalry, idolatry, and "us versus them" identities. Causes replaced repentance. Flags replaced humility. Truth is no longer received — it is claimed.

So again, the question is not whether unity or division is good.

The question is:

Who rules the unity?

And who is worshiped in the division?

Until we return to the center — until truth has a Name again — our world will continue to oscillate between domination and fragmentation, calling both "progress," while repeating the same ancient rebellion.

Because our Creator is not:

"I am what your culture approves,"

not "I am what your trauma demands,"

not "I am whatever you interpreted today."

He is I AM.

CHAPTER 5

Pain as Proof of Life

It is not my aim to untangle every thread of how humanity arrived at the brokenness we now inhabit. Greater minds than mine have devoted their lives to that question. I write instead of a simpler necessity: the need to name what I lived without yet understanding it. Growth often begins this way—not with certainty, but with the courage to wrestle honestly with what we do not yet comprehend.

"All roads lead to Rome," the saying goes. But what you see when you arrive depends entirely on what you believe Rome is.

***

I remember my first visit to house-church. Someone asked a gentle, disarming question meant to break the ice:

"What is one trait you inherited from your parents that you would like to keep?"

As the question circled the room, I sank into my chair, flooded with quiet shame. I could not name a single trait — neither because my parents had none, nor because I had none, but because I could not see goodness anywhere in myself. That single question exposed what my entire life had been constructed to conceal.

I had been gripping my past with such force that it drained all my life forward. And yet my past was not a refuge of warmth or nostalgia. It was darker than my present — always. Why, then, did I cling to it?

The answer had been with me for years. I had written it at eighteen and later carved it onto my wall:

"My pain tells me that I am alive."

At the time, I did not understand what I was confessing. I was so hollowed out that pain had become my only evidence of existence. I sought it — not consciously, but faithfully —because I feared that without pain, I would disappear altogether.

I knew many things then. I read philosophy. I analyzed suffering. I spoke fluently about death, meaning, and existence. But knowing is not the same as understanding, and understanding is not the same as being healed. Knowledge did not rescue me. It kept me functioning.

My rebellion was not strength.

It was starvation.

***

Looking back, I want to reach my younger self — to tell her that God was present even when she felt abandoned. But I know she would not believe me. Loneliness is persuasive. And it never travels alone. Emptiness walks beside it, loyal and patient.

***

Like many, I learned early to measure myself against others. Comparison masqueraded as motivation, but it functioned as a ceiling. I could see only as high as someone else had already climbed. It also became a hiding place — a way to justify stagnation, to preserve fear under the language of humility.

We are taught to honor our roots: history, tradition, values, identity. These can be anchors — but they can also become excuses. The same structures meant to preserve life can be used to defend inertia, incompetence, or manipulation.

When those inherited walls felt too tight, I broke them. I adopted more flexible ideas, called them progress, and congratulated myself for growth — only to discover I had built yet another ceiling.

I believed freedom meant self-sufficiency. Independence. Standing alone.

My definitions were sophisticated.

They were also still chained to fear.

In those years, I hovered between atheism and agnosticism. I admired Sisyphus — the image of dignity through defiance, meaning extracted from absurdity. Suffering embraced without surrender. I mistook endurance for transcendence.

Everything became symbolic. Historical figures. Literary heroes. Places. Objects. Even God.

Yes — God was a symbol in my vocabulary.

I emptied my spirituality instead of filling it. I prided myself on being "spiritual, not religious," unaware that both, belief and disbelief, require faith. There is no neutral ground. We either build our lives on God's presence or on His absence.

Rome awaits either way.

***

What I did not understand then was that freedom does not exist without boundaries. Without limitation, freedom collapses into meaninglessness. And freedom cannot survive in isolation. We are not designed to bear ourselves alone. True freedom is relational. It flourishes within love, not autonomy.

Only later did I understand that self-sufficiency was not liberation — it was voluntary captivity.

In God, freedom does not remove limits; it restores purpose. He does not eliminate dependence; He reorders it. In Christ, freedom is not the absence of restraint, but the presence of truth.

***

"My pain tells me that I am alive."

The sentence haunted me for most of my life because pain is not only something we endure. It is a sign.

A sign of rupture.

Of fracture.

Of separation.

I once believed pain proved God's absence. Now I know it reveals a broken relationship — and an invitation to be restored.

Pain is what reality feels like when it is not whole.

And grace is what meets us there — not to erase pain, but to redeem it.

CHAPTER 6

HIS Story vs History

Napoleon once said, *"History is a set of lies agreed upon."*

He spoke as a man who understood conquest, memory, and power — how easily truth bends when survival, pride, or victory is at stake. The victors rewrite the story. The wounded forget what they cannot bear. And the world moves forward calling distortion peace.

That sentence finds its ancient echo in Genesis, in the first agreed-upon lie ever spoken:

"You will not surely die." (Genesis 3:4)

That was not merely deception — it was **revisionism**. A rewriting of reality to remove consequences. Since then, humanity has repeated the same instinct across civilizations, religions, and personal lives: deny the wound, redefine the cost, forget the healer.

And this is not only the history of nations.

It is the history of the human heart.

We curate our own narratives. We edit out what shames us, soften what convicts us, rename what exposes us. Pain becomes something to hide, medicate, distract from, or explain away. Slowly, the story of who we are turns into our own "set of lies we agree upon" — a version of history tidy enough to survive, but too thin to heal.

Pain was never the enemy.

It was designed as a messenger.

Pain announces rupture — separation from what sustains life. Yet we call it cruelty and build entire cultures around escaping it. The modern world has mastered this craft. We drown pain in noise, anesthetize it with consumption, philosophize it into irrelevance. We call avoidance wisdom. We call numbness progress.

In truth, this instinct began in Eden — the internal withdrawal that made the physical act inevitable. We hid our hearts behind the veil of doubt before we ever reached for the fruit. The rebellion wasn't just the bite; it was the moment we leaned into the whisper of the serpent and agreed to a reality where God's word was negotiable. We chose to be our own gods in the dark, and the eating was simply the manifestation of that choice.

Once we preferred the shadow to the Substance, we became inhabitants of the dimness. Plato captured this human condition with haunting clarity in *The Allegory of the Cave.*

A group of people are born chained inside a cavern, their necks fixed, their gaze locked on the stone wall before them. Behind them a fire burns. Between the fire and the prisoners, figures pass — casting shadows on the wall.

The prisoners name the shadows. Debate them. Build meaning around them. This is all they have ever known. To them, the shadows are reality.

Then one prisoner is freed.

At first, he is forced to turn toward the fire. The light sears his eyes. It disorients him. Everything he once believed collapses under the weight of brightness. He resists. He longs for the familiar comfort of illusion.

But he is led further — out of the cave.

There, under the open sky, his eyes slowly awaken. He sees colors, depth, distance, life. The sun reveals what the fire never could. And suddenly, the truth becomes unbearable in its beauty.

Overwhelmed with wonder — and grief — he returns to the cave to tell the others. He speaks of the exit. Of the sky. Of a world more real than pain.

They do not listen.

Their eyes recoil. Their beliefs defend themselves. They mock him. They insist the cave is all there is. And if he attempts to free them, they are prepared to silence him forever.

Because nothing threatens a false truth more than the light that exposes it.

When truth approaches, it hurts. Not because it is cruel — but because it unmasks illusion. Every age invents its anesthetics: power, ideology, pleasure, denial. We convince ourselves that avoiding pain is wisdom, but in reality, it is bondage.

When Christ said, *"You shall know the truth, and the truth shall make you free,"* (John 8:32). He was not promising comfort. He was promising **wholeness.**

Freedom is not the absence of pain.

It is the presence of truth.

Perhaps Napoleon was right — human history is memory shaped by fear, politics, and survival. But God's story is different. His truth is not negotiated, edited, or revised. It is offered — again and again — to a world terrified of remembering.

And when we allow God to re-write our stories, truth does not destroy us. It resurrects us.

The pain we feared becomes proof of life returning.

Illusion dissolves.

And for the first time, we see — not history, but **His Story.**

CHAPTER 7

Why God Speaks in History

The Bible is not God entering history. It is God refusing to let history redefine Him.

Before the written Word, God governed humanity through conscience, creation, consequence, memory of encounter, and covenant. Scripture does not invent morality — it names what already existed.

From the beginning, humanity is portrayed as created in God's image — capable of obedience, aware of right and wrong. No written law exists when Cain murders his brother. Yet Cain knows his act is evil. God confronts him. Cain is judged. Moral awareness predates codified commandment.

Creation itself functions as revelation. Order, power, dependence — these are communicated through the natural world. This is why ancient cultures revere the sky, fear storms, honor the sun. They respond to real signals — but misinterpret them.

Creation points to God.

It was never meant to replace Him.

Conscience functions as moral witness — the law written on the heart. Across civilizations, prohibitions against murder, betrayal, and injustice emerge independently. God never left humanity morally ungoverned.

Paul names this reality plainly:

"They show that the work of the law is written on their hearts, while their conscience also bears witness." (Romans 2:15)

Before written law, consequence taught. Violence produced chaos. Pride produced collapse. Exploitation produced suffering. The Flood narrative is not about rule-breaking — it is about a world unraveling under its own moral weight. Judgment, in Scripture, is often containment rather than annihilation.

Ancient myths are not dismissed by the Bible as fiction. They are understood as *fractured memory* — truth refracted through culture and time. Flood stories appear globally. Sacrifices recur everywhere. Judgment and moral order echo across civilizations.

Scripture does not deny these memories.

It corrects them.

God's earliest covenants are universal, not textual. The covenant with Noah binds God to all humanity — preserving life, setting moral boundaries — without written law. His faithfulness does not depend on literacy.

So why does Scripture appear "late"?

Because humanity was not ready. Literacy was limited. Social structures were unstable. Moral awareness existed — but fragmented. The Law does not create morality. It stabilizes it.

This explains why Scripture regulates existing practices rather than erasing them instantly. God works *redemptively*, not abstractly. Instead of forcing moral perfection, He enters history, confronts evil gradually, restrains harm, and redirects conscience over time.

Humanity did not begin in religious confusion — it began in direct awareness. People knew God, then distorted that knowledge. Instead of one God over all, humanity fractured transcendence:

God of rain.

God of war.

God of fertility.

God of borders.

This was not revelation expanding — it was revelation breaking apart. Humanity did not merely misunderstand God — it recreated Him.

The perfect wholeness of Creation became the curated reality of the "cave." Observing it from the outside, most religions and philosophies at our disposal are simply sophisticated maps of the darkness in the cavern. They are human-made techniques created to navigate the fracture.

Buddhism offers a map of elimination, teaching the prisoner how to detach from the pain of the chains.

Islam offers a map of submission, providing a rigorous code of conduct to live righteously while still inside the cave.

Yoga, Krishna, and contemporary philosophies offer instructions on how to interpret the flickering figures on the wall or how to sit in the chains with more dignity.

They all point toward a "Right Path" or a "Higher Truth," but a map of the dark is not the same thing as the Light. The Buddha is a teacher of the map; Muhammad is a prophet of the code. They remain external to the truth they describe.

God allows false gods to persist — not because truth is weak, but because freedom is real...

CHAPTER 8

Addiction to Pain

My hiStory between the lines (Part I)

As a child, I was chubby — not outright ugly, but certainly far from attractive, at least in my own eyes. My relationship with food was indifferent; there was little variety during my upbringing, and preference was not something I learned to expect. I cannot say I went hungry, but abundance was never part of my world either. My wardrobe was sparse — mostly my school uniform, and a navy-blue dress with a crisp white shirt that still stands out in my memory. I did not own my first pair of jeans until ninth grade.

When my parents, who were working in Libya at the time, bought me clothes from Korecom — a chain of duty-free stores in Bulgaria accessible only with convertible foreign currency — I was seen as a lucky girl. Shopping there carried prestige. Yet I was not the one who chose those clothes. They were beautiful, tasteful, and expensive. Among them were the long-desired Wrangler jeans.

My father had impeccable taste. He was always well dressed — tailored suits, ironed shirts, polished shoes. He was also exceptionally intelligent — smarter, he believed, than anyone else around him. In his mind, that intelligence granted him authority. He knew what I should wear, when I should go out, who my friends should be, which relatives mattered, how I should speak, what I should study, even who I should love. He was, without a doubt, an erudite man.

My mother is far harder to place in my childhood memories. It was my grandmother who raised me until seventh grade. I remember my mother visiting occasionally, but my grandmother often forbade me from opening the door. Later, she would retrieve the bags my mother had left with the neighbors, but I rarely saw their contents. Most of it went straight into the trash, along with my grandmother's stern explanation that my mother was a disgrace and that I needed nothing from her.

I do not have many warm memories of my grandmother. There are a few humorous moments from summers in Sliven[4], but little else. One incident though, stands out sharply.

After one of my mother's attempted visits, I retrieved a skirt she had bought me from the trash and hid it. It was long, dark red, woven. The next day, I wore it to school, tucking it into my bag to avoid being seen. I forgot to change before returning home.

When my grandmother saw me, she flew into a rage. She stripped the skirt off me and whipped me with a large black umbrella. But it was not the beating, nor the shouting, nor the words that left the deepest mark.

In our hallway, we had a rug made from goat hair — a *kozyak.* White, gray, and black. Goat hair is sharp, shedding tiny fibers that embed themselves into fabric and are nearly impossible to remove. What remains most vivid in my memory is my grandmother furiously wiping the rug with my red skirt, turning it inside out, grinding the hairs in, making sure not a single spot was spared.

If you were to ask me then, I would say my grandmother did not believe in God. Neither did my father. As for me, God was not even a concept. Not because I had not heard of God — I had heard of many gods. To me, they were metaphors, human inventions meant to explain an incomprehensible world. They were stories. Greek mythology drew me in deeply. Later, Buddhism and Hare Krishna. Yet I never sought out the story of Christ. And still, Golgotha stood as the most powerful symbol in my mind, resonating far more deeply than anything I could explain.

That alone should give one pause.

***

Now fast forward to Bulgaria between 1991 and 1995 — a time of upheaval and collapse. I was twenty-two, and everything familiar was unraveling. In those four years, I immigrated to Germany, narrowly escaped being raped, met the man who would become the father of my children, fell in love, became pregnant, was introduced to God and Jesus — and discovered that the man I loved was abusive. I returned to Bulgaria, bare-

4. city in Bulgaria

ly escaped human traffickers, became an investigative reporter, had my face shattered by the same man I dearly loved, was betrayed by him and my closest childhood friend, and finally had an encounter with the Devil himself.

What stands out in this period is not the number of events, but the pattern: pain looping back on itself, each cycle deeper than the last. Instead of escape, there was escalation. Pain was becoming my existence — my identity, my orientation, my certainty in an otherwise empty world. Without it, I felt I would disappear.

Written now, it sounds implausible, almost literary. But it is not fiction. When pain is used to create identity, loyalty, and control, it becomes addictive — not only personally, but socially. And this is how the circle closes.

***

To understand this, context matters.

Bulgaria was transitioning from communism to democracy and a market economy. Prices skyrocketed. Corruption flourished. Privatization enriched a few while devastating many. Organized crime filled the vacuum left by collapsing institutions. A new class emerged — *mutri* — synonymous with racketeering, extortion, and violence. Fear became normalized.

Like many others, I sought a way out. With no financial means, Germany was the closest option. I shared my plan with my best friend Lily. We were inseparable since kindergarten — neighbors, classmates, sisters in everything but blood. We shared food, beds, secrets, even bathrooms. There was no one I trusted more.

Lily came from a much wealthier family than me. She never worried about allowance, food, or clothes. But more than money, she had freedom. No curfew. No need to ask permission to go to the movies. She even decided to start working and leave school in seventh grade. I was jealous — quietly, privately — but I admired her.

And she was beautiful. Truly beautiful. Slim, with a flat stomach, small but perfectly formed breasts, huge hazel eyes, and thick golden hair falling in heavy waves over her shoulders. She also had a natural gift for makeup — the kind that transforms without effort.

When I told Lily about my plan to emigrate, she decided to come with me. The feeling was intoxicating. Two best friends, starting an adventure, taking on the world together. We set a date. I sold everything I had of value — the diamond earrings and necklace from my prom (a story I tell in *The Faces of Unborn Butterflies*), my DVD player, most of my Korecom clothes — and finally gathered enough money for a plane ticket.

It was summer. June or July — I don't remember exactly. I wore a sailor suit custom tailored just a month before we left. I still have a photograph from the Berlin airport: I look like a happy child-captain, sunlight in my eyes. A long white skirt flowed like a tide around my legs, pleated softly, brushing my ankles. A deep navy-blue jacket hugged my frame, its polished buttons lined up like small anchors. The broad lapels echoed a sailor's collar — promises of voyages and untold adventures.

I was ready.

We landed in East Berlin and crossed into West Berlin by U-Bahn.[5] In 1991, that journey was more than transportation — it was a passage through history. The trains rumbled through tunnels once sealed during the Cold War. In the East, stations were dim and austere, marked by peeling paint and faded signs — remnants of the ghost stations trains once passed without stopping. As we crossed into the West, everything shifted. The stations grew brighter, more colorful. Advertisements replaced propaganda. Passengers blended — some still adjusting to reunification, others long accustomed to Western comfort. Above ground, fragments of the Wall still stood.

It felt exactly as it should have — adrenaline, hope, bold plans. The U-Bahn carried with it the echoes of my divided past and the promise that the scars might finally heal.

Reality intervened quickly.

By the time we reached our station, it was after 7 p.m. The tourist agency where I had arranged our accommodation was closed. Lily suggested a hotel. I knew I couldn't afford it. As panic crept in, a man in his

5. the German equivalent of a subway or metro system

thirties approached us — dark-haired, smiling, disarmingly friendly. He asked if we were looking for a place to stay. Desperation made us hopeful. After agreeing on a price, we followed him onto another U-Bahn train.

The journey lasted nearly forty minutes, followed by a long walk through unfamiliar streets. Hungry and exhausted, we dragged our suitcases until we reached an old building with unsettling architecture. Inside, the corridors twisted like a labyrinth. The apartment was dark. In the living room, lit only by a flickering television, a man sat in a high-backed leather chair, his silhouette heavy, watching us. The man who brought us spoke to him in a language we did not understand.

We were shown a fridge, offered coffee and croissants, then led to a small room with two doors. One leading to the hallway; the other, we were told, was a connection to an adjoining room — locked, they assured us. No key was given. The air felt tight.

As Lily unpacked, the dark-haired man smiled wider. "I see you're eager to take a shower," he said, his eyes lingering. He pointed out the bathroom, then turned to me.

"Does your friend have a boyfriend?"

I nodded, my heart pounding.

"She's very beautiful," he added. "When she's done, tell her to join us for coffee while she waits for you."

The moment he left, I packed Lily's belongings back into her suitcase. I knocked on the bathroom door and told her everything. Our room was on the first floor. I opened the window, threw our bags out, and helped her climb down. I told her to call for help if I wasn't back in ten minutes.

They refused to return our money, but they let me leave.

At ten in the evening, we stood on the streets of West Berlin — two frightened twenty-two-year-old girls with suitcases and nowhere to go. We wandered for hours until Lily, broken and exhausted, decided to return to Bulgaria. She took a taxi to the airport and exchanged her ticket for the earliest flight home.

I understood her choice, but the realization of our different realities was a cold blade. She had a round-trip ticket; mine was one-way. Worse was the careless cruelty of her departure: at the airport, she spent over two hundred German marks on gifts for the family she was returning to, knowing she was leaving me behind in a foreign country, alone, with only fifty marks to my name.

I felt more than abandoned — I felt betrayed. She was casually shopping, while I was standing on the edge of a world that didn't know I existed.

The next day, I took the U-Bahn to the Federal Office for Migration and Refugees, wounded, scared, but determined.

The pain felt familiar. Predictable. Reliable.

It was not something I suffered.

It was something I used — to orient myself, to feel real, to prove existence.

Pain became the only thing that answered me back.

That is how every addiction begins.

CHAPTER 9

Addiction to Pain

My hiStory between the lines (Part II)

"'Unless you people see signs and wonders,' Jesus told him, 'you will never believe.'"— John 4:48 (NIV)

"Please, God, let me get through this today," I whispered, standing in the endless three-fold line in front of the Federal Office of Migration. The queue stretched like a living thing — coiling, shifting, swallowing the morning hours. I knew the office would close in seven hours. I also knew there was a real chance my turn would never come.

The idea of spending the night outside, guarding my place on the pavement, felt unbearable. My suitcase pulled onto my shoulder. My stomach burned with hunger. I kept murmuring *"Please, God,"* though I did not truly believe anyone was listening.

Why would God care about someone like me? And was there a God at all — or only a story humanity told itself when fear grew too heavy?

The hours passed. My legs weakened. Dizziness crept in. I asked the woman behind me to hold my place and shuffled toward a food stand. The smell of ham sandwiches and spinning meat made my hunger ache. I counted my coins and bought what I could: two bottles of water, a small coffee, and a croissant.

On my way back, I heard something that stopped me cold — Bulgarian. My native language, spoken softly nearby, cut through the noise like a rope thrown to a drowning person. I approached the two men immediately. The older one was distant, almost hostile. The younger one — Ivan — was different. He listened. He explained the asylum process patiently: acceptance, then an immigration camp, then housing while paperwork crawled forward.

When Ivan learned I had no money and nowhere to stay, he did something extraordinary. He offered to sneak me into his camp. He gave me his bunk. He handed me his dinner, saying he had already eaten while waiting outside.

I thanked Ivan.

I did not thank God.

In that moment, Ivan became my savior, and I forgot the prayers I had whispered hours earlier. This is one of the great contradictions of the human heart: when rescue comes through people, we call it kindness or luck; when suffering comes, we demand explanations from God.

***

After a long and exhausting process, I was placed in a small village called Meidelshtetten, tucked into the rolling hills of the Swabian Jura. The landscape was ancient and quiet — cliffs and valleys holding their breath. Especially when the lavender bloomed, the world felt suspended in calm.

And yet, I was desperately lonely.

One evening, I went to a nearby pub, hungry for human presence. There, I met a young man with dark, shoulder-length hair and mischievous eyes. We talked. We laughed. We danced. For the first time in what felt like forever, I felt alive.

His name was Roman and he was from Romania. We shared fragments of Eastern Europe, of displacement, of familiarity. For weeks we met almost daily. Then he told me he was being transferred. Before leaving, he invited me to celebrate his birthday with friends from the asylum home.

I said yes.

The night began simply — food, drinks, music, laughter. Time just flew. It was already too dark to walk back home, so Roman offered me his room. I trusted him. I had feelings for him. I agreed.

Later that night, I woke up and went to the restroom. On my way back, an older man stepped out of his room. He grabbed my arm and demanded to know where I was going. Before I could answer, he slapped me hard across the face and called me a whore.

Then he opened his door and said it was now everyone else's turn.

Inside the dim room were fifteen men. Roman sat in a corner, unable to meet my eyes. I was forced to my knees in the center. Faces closed in. Pants unzipped. Orders barked in a language I could barely register.

Fear hollowed me out. I could not scream. I could not think. My body froze. But somehow, I lifted my head and looked at the man in front of me. I don't know where the words came from.

"Please," I said. "What if I were your sister?"

Something shifted. His face changed. He zipped his pants, wiped his forehead, pulled me up, and pushed me out of the room. Without speaking, he drove me back to my village. When I got out of the car, he muttered a rough apology.

I never saw him — or Roman — again.

***

Years later, back in Bulgaria, I was a single mother of two, working as a hostess in Sunny Beach. The job was seasonal but well paid. I needed it.

I shared a room with Kalina, a gentle young woman my age. One night, a group of men stayed long after closing. We suspected they were mutri—mafia. The owner insisted we accommodate them.

Most were drunk and aggressive. Two seemed sober, even polite.

When the night ended, Kalina and I prepared to head home, but the last bus had already left. It was a warm, breezy night, and we didn't mind walking. As we strolled along the dark road, a luxury Mercedes-Benz suddenly pulled up beside us. The tinted window rolled down to reveal the smiling face of one of the men from the restaurant — the "nice" one who had apologized earlier for his friends' behavior. He offered us a ride.

We accepted.

Instead of taking us home, he drove to a bar called Neptun. Inside, only a bartender and two men sat drinking vodka. One of them smiled at us and asked what we wanted to drink.

I said we weren't thirsty.

He pulled out a gun.

The barrel pointed at me as he laughed. "I bet you want a drink now."

Then he slammed the gun onto the bar. "Just kidding."

Money appeared. Phones rang. More men arrived. The air thickened.

Finally, the "nice guy" turned to us, offering a flimsy apology. "Let's go, girls. Sorry about all this. Don't mind him; he's just drunk," he said, nodding towards the gunman. His words barely registered as all I wanted was to escape the suffocating danger of that place. We hastily made our way to the car, but no sooner had we settled in the back seat than two large men slid in beside us, trapping us between them. The car doors closed with a decisive click, sealing our fate for the night.

We were taken to a villa in Saint Vlas, a notorious seaside resort infamous for its association with the Bulgarian racketeering mafia. As we entered, a woman, clearly under some influence, pressed a drink into my hand and whispered urgently, "What are you doing here? Run."

Her words sent a shiver down my spine. Fear gripped me, paralyzing my thoughts. I glanced at Kalina, whose eyes mirrored my own terror, but we were both too scared and confused to act immediately. Instead, we found ourselves observing the unsettling scene unfolding around us. Men armed with pistols and rifles moved in and out of the villa, their conversations a mix of hushed tones and sharp commands. Time and again, they glanced our way, their eyes gleaming with something dark and dangerous. Occasionally, they would throw a belittling remark in our direction, thinly veiled as a compliment, or they would urge us to drink more, as if to dull our senses to the reality of the situation.

The windows were shut tight with heavy wooden blinds, locked from the inside, and the only visible exit was the front door — a door that now seemed a million miles away. We searched for the woman who had warned us, but she had disappeared upstairs hours ago, leaving us alone in this den of lingering threats. The realization slowly dawned on us: we might never see our families or friends again.

The first chance we had to escape came in the living room. Left alone for just a moment, we bolted for the door. But as soon as we stepped outside, we were hit by the stark reality that the villa was situated on the main road, up and down - nothing but open fields. Panic overtook us as we darted between villas, hiding behind cars and buildings, desperately knocking on doors, hoping someone — anyone — would help us. But door after door remained closed. In those days, no one wanted anything to do with the 'mutri.'

Finally, we reached a small bungalow. We banged on the door with all our strength, and after what felt like an eternity, a sleepy man answered. We poured out our story in frantic, terrified words, our fear palpable. Seeing our desperation, he agreed to help. He checked to make sure no one was watching, then unlocked his old truck and opened the back door. Kalina and I clambered inside, hearts pounding, as he drove us to the bus station in Sunny Beach.

To our shock and horror, mere minutes after he dropped us off, the same black Mercedes Benz that had taken us to the villa pulled up beside us. The door swung open, and we were ordered to get inside. The pit of despair was opening beneath us once more when, by what I can only describe as divine intervention, a police car pulled up behind the Mercedes. Two officers stepped out to buy coffee from the bus stop's stand, and in that brief moment of distraction, we seized our chance. We ran into the bus station, boarded the first bus to Burgas, and didn't look back.

That night, we lost our well-paying seasonal jobs, but we gained something far more precious — our lives. But did we thank Jesus for this miraculous escape? I'm not sure we ever did.

"The Pharisees came and began to question Jesus. To test him, they asked him for a sign from heaven." Mark 8:11

"Then Jesus told him, 'Because you have seen me, you have believed; blessed are those who have not seen and yet have believed.'" John 20:29

How strange, self-absorbed, and ungrateful we humans can be. We demand signs and miracles, and when they aren't handed to us on a silver platter, we grow angry and deny God's existence. When miracles do grace our lives, we often fail to see them or refuse to acknowledge their divine origin. We fear what we cannot explain, or we shy away from faith, worried about what others might think. And so, we run — from God, from belief, from the very miracles that are meant to guide and save us.

I ran too.

But He refused to let me go.

CHAPTER 10

Fate and Faith

Germany, 1991.

I was living with the love of my life, Boris, in a small room — one of two rooms in a modest bungalow reserved for immigrant families. The other room belonged to an African family with three children. We shared a single bathroom and a narrow kitchen, all of us waiting with the same fragile hope — that one day we might be assigned one of the tiny houses promised to families like ours.

That was the season when the dreams began.

The first dream visited me repeatedly for years.

I was trapped in a white room — no doors, no windows. I could not move. I could not speak. My body felt heavy, paralyzed, as if the air itself had hardened around me. Then they appeared: white, faceless zombies, advancing slowly, deliberately. And I understood something with terrifying clarity — they were coming for my eyes. My brown eyes. The only color in the dream. The only thing that made me, *me.*

Around the same time, a second dream entered my nights — entirely different, yet just as vivid.

I was swimming in the ocean. Not struggling, not floating, but moving freely beneath the surface of vast, azure waters. Above me, the sun cast its light through the waves, forming a luminous path that seemed meant for me alone. The underwater world opened around me like a hidden kingdom — coral gardens shimmering with color, schools of silver fish gliding past like living constellations, currents humming with quiet power. Everything felt alive, ancient, and welcoming, as if the ocean itself recognized me and breathed with my lungs.

I swam deeper and deeper, drawn by unknown inviting hand.

And there, hidden beyond world's reach, I found a small chest. It was modest, unadorned, and yet, magnetic. I opened it and inside lay a pearl unlike anything I had ever seen — perfect, luminous, impossibly pure, gentle and absolute.

When I took the pearl in my hand, its light filled me, and from its core flowed something unmistakable — love. Steady, encompassing, alive. I closed my fist around it and began swimming back toward the surface, guarding it with everything in me.

The moment I emerged from the ocean, the sky turned black. Darkness swallowed the horizon. The wind rose suddenly, violent and raging. I could not see them, but I could feel them — an immense, advancing horde. The air thickened with the stench of iron and decay. I heard the pounding of countless feet, the roar of something ancient and merciless gathering force behind me.

I ran.

I ran with the pearl clenched in my fist, my heart pounding, despair tightening my chest. I could feel the enemy drawing closer — their breath, their reaching arms, the certainty of pursuit. Terror overtook me. I knew I could not outrun them. I could not fight them.

Exhausted, I turned to face what was coming.

I dropped to my knees. I closed my eyes. I waited.

And then I saw Him.

A white stallion descended from the open sky — majestic, radiant, divine. His chest was massive and powerful; his muscles carved with strength beyond anything earthly. His mane flowed like living light in the wind. His eyes burned with intelligence and authority, and his nostrils flared as if drawing in the weight of the world itself.

He landed directly in front of me — just as thousands of swords came crashing down.

The blades struck His chest.

I saw a single, thin red line appear. Blood flowed down, bright against the white, forming a perfect cross.

And then I woke up.

***

Only much later did I understand that both dreams were telling the same story: something precious was being entrusted to me, and I was never meant to carry it by my own strength.

***

Not long after those dreams, I and Boris met a family – Krasi and Veselina - with two children, the wife pregnant with their third. They dreamed of having seven children. I was eight and a half months pregnant with my first son. This family introduced us to God — not as an idea or philosophy, but as reality. Reality in Jesus.

I will never forget our baptism.

December 1991.

A gloomy, cold day in Germany. We stood barefoot, shivering by the scenic banks of Lauchert river in Baden-Württemberg. I wore my favorite white silk pajamas, and Veselina gave me one of her jackets — pink, warm, a small burst of color against the gray sky. Despite the cold, Boris and I smiled as we stepped into the freezing water. The husband, Krasi, submerged us in the name of Jesus.

Later, we celebrated in their home. I can still see the kitchen — small and cozy, filled with warmth, the scent of freshly baked bread and vanilla. After lunch, they asked if we wanted to pray to be baptized with the Holy Spirit, explaining that we might receive the gift of tongues — a heavenly language.

We sat on the floor, holding hands.

At first the prayer was gentle, quiet. Then it grew in passion. And suddenly, in that tiny kitchen, with all doors and windows closed, I felt a breeze brush my face. Soft. Cool. Alive. My hair moved as if touched by spring itself. It carried peace, kindness, love — something utterly unlike anything I had ever known.

Words began flowing from my mouth — words I did not understand yet felt profoundly real.

And then fear settled in.

I pulled away.

Yes. I rejected the gift of God.

Grace had reached me but surrender still frightened me more than pain.

***

Life rushed forward. I gave birth to my first son. Three months later, I sent him away.

At the time, it seemed practical. Boris and I both needed to work. We needed money. We told ourselves it was temporary, necessary, even responsible. My mother would take care of our baby in Bulgaria until we saved enough to return home.

I remember holding my son before he left — his weight still unfamiliar in my arms, his smell already woven into my soul. I told myself he was too young to remember. I told myself love could stretch across distance. I told myself I was doing the right thing.

What I felt that day at the airport was pain — sharp, animal pain that hollowed me out. What he felt was something deeper: abandonment. And just because I did not intend it, just because I was ignorant of it, does not mean the wound did not form.

Ignorance does not excuse consequences. Love without submission to God easily mistakes necessity for wisdom. Living in the absence of God teaches us to solve spiritual hunger with logistical solutions. It convinces us we can manage life on our own.

We cannot.

***

After that, everything between Boris and me began to unravel. The tenderness faded at first. Then trust. Then safety.

I became pregnant with our second son, and instead of joy, accusations followed. I was told the child was not his. Words became weapons. Silence became punishment. And then came the first violent outburst.

I wish I could say that moment drove me back to God. It did not. I relied on myself. On endurance, explanation, reinterpretation. On survival.

God kept extending his hand - again and again. He held me in His arms when I collapsed. He breathed life into my lungs when I could barely breathe. He covered me with grace I did not deserve. And I behaved as if He did not exist.

There is a peculiar arrogance in suffering without God. We mistake endurance for strength. Survival for wisdom. Control for safety.

And the cost is always higher than we can ever imagine.

***

Eventually, the weight of everything — fear, shame, exhaustion, denial — became unbearable. So, I did what so many of us do when reality presses too hard. I ran.

I returned to Bulgaria. Boris said he would stay in Germany a few more months to save money. That explanation felt thin even then, but I accepted it because acceptance was easier than confrontation. This story sounds ordinary, doesn't it? Many families fracture this way. Many endure far worse. I am not telling you this to claim uniqueness, but to offer context. Because what came next cannot be understood without what was before.

***

Christmas Eve, 1992

I arrived in Burgas in early December and surprised my mother—and my ten-and-a-half-month-old son. Tears. Laughter. Disbelief. The familiar chaos of reunion.

On December 22, my friend Lily and I traveled to Sofia. I felt it was my duty to introduce my son to his other grandparents. Lily came along, planning to spend time with her boyfriend.

On December 24, we met my cousin at a café near the Pliska Hotel bus station. Coffee turned into conversation. Conversation into laughter.

And then — we missed the bus.

The only bus.

We were stranded in Sofia on Christmas Eve.

Trying to make the best of it, we bought beans, flour, wine, and nuts, and went to Lily's apartment to prepare a traditional Christmas Eve dinner — to celebrate anyway.

I need to pause here to explain something important.

Lily was deeply involved in extrasensory practices — psychic training, future-telling, and mystical painting. Her apartment reflected that world. The walls were covered with paintings of distorted faces, third eyes, pentagrams — symbols that made the air feel heavy. Pressurized. As if the room itself was holding its breath.

The apartment was small — a studio with one room, a narrow hallway, and a cramped kitchen. I put my baby to sleep in the only room. The four adults — Lily, her boyfriend, my cousin, and I — gathered in the kitchen.

We tried to cook the beans. They burned.

We tried to bake the bread. It burned too.

We laughed awkwardly, poured wine, cracked nuts. I drank juice, my pregnant belly reminding me that life was still growing inside me.

Then Lily told a story.

She spoke of a psychic instructor who claimed the Devil could hide even in paintings of Jesus. She described seeing a crucifix transform — Christ's foot becoming a horse's hoof, a tail curling behind the cross, the Devil's face smiling through the wood. She warned us that faith alone was not enough. That we needed amulets. Protection. Because evil, she said, was stronger than we could imagine.

I disagreed.

I said faith alone is enough.

That God is stronger than evil.

That true belief needs no objects.

We debated.

And then my son screamed.

He did not cry — he screamed.

I ran into the room and lifted him, trying to soothe him. Each time I laid him down and stepped away, the screams returned — primal, unbearable, as if something were tearing him open from the inside. I moved back and forth between the kitchen and the room with the paintings, rocking him, whispering, still arguing with Lily across the doorway.

And then —

I was holding my baby, swaying him, singing softly, when his eyes began to change.

They narrowed.

Turned yellow.

Vertical pupils.

Glowing.

His cry twisted into laughter —cold, mocking, inhuman. His teeth seemed to grow. His face — my baby's face — became something else. Something horrifying.

And a voice filled my mind.

Rhythmic. Commanding. Relentless.

This is the Devil. Kill the Devil.

Grab him by his feet and smash his head into the wall.

It is your responsibility! Kill the Devil!

The terror is impossible to describe. Every instinct screamed obedience — until something deeper broke through.

I screamed:

"In the name of Jesus! This is my son!"

Again, and again, and again. I screamed.

When my cousin burst into the room, the vision vanished.

My baby was still in my arms. But his thighs and arms were bruised — blue fingerprints burned into his skin by my grip. I had pressed him to my chest with everything I had.

And I know this now:

it would not have been enough —

if Jesus had not been there.

But when it was over — did I fall to my knees in gratitude?

No.

I reduced Jesus once again to a symbol. A trigger for my strength. A power I could summon whenever needed. I used His name as a tool.

I told the story carefully. Hesitantly. To very few people. And when I did, I framed it as a warning about evil — not as testimony to salvation. I worried about how people would see me. God was not the center.

I was.

Only much later did I understand what I could not see then: I chose my addiction — survival, compartmentalization, continuation. I chose the familiar ache of a fractured world over surrender.

I chose known suffering — because it felt safer than trust.

***

Pain — we cling to it because we have learned to define ourselves through it. We use it as a milestone of endurance, a test of character, a measurement of our greatness. It becomes proof that we are strong, capable, unbreakable. If pain were to vanish suddenly, most of us would lose our compass. Without something to fight, we would not know who we are. Pain is the familiar choice, often masqueraded as safety.

Perhaps that is why it feels easier to reject a God who offers *transformation.* Transformation requires surrender — and surrender feels like death to the self we've built around our wounds. But God asks us to release the control of familiarity and step into the Unknown — the very place where we feel unsafe, insecure, weak, and alone.

What we fail to see is that our fear of the Unknown exists only because we resist God. The moment we accept that He exists — and recognize that His power is guided by love, not domination — everything changes. For if God, the Creator of all, has the power to do whatever He wills, yet chooses patience, mercy, and sacrifice — then He cannot be our enemy.

He suffers with us, and even more astonishingly, He suffers *for* us.

Once we connect these truths, the Unknown ceases to be frightening. And when the Unknown loses its terror, pain loses its grip. That is where transformation begins — not in escaping pain, but in allowing it to become the sacred place where fear dies and faith is born.

Every moment I trusted my own strength, my own wisdom, my own explanations, my path bent toward destruction. Every moment I ignored God's outstretched hand, I did not escape consequence — I simply chose it.

And in the end, I learned the truth that binds every moment of this story together:

Faith is not a belief without cost.

Faith is direction.

Faith is what shapes our fate.

CHAPTER 11

The First Wound

"And the LORD God commanded the man, 'You are free to eat from any tree in the garden; but you must not eat from the tree of the knowledge of good and evil, for when you eat from it you will certainly die" (Genesis 2:16–17 (NIV)

Genesis 2 and 3 mark the moment where everything — shattered truth, misplaced authority, fractured identity, pride, division, pain—enters history. This is not merely a story about disobedience. It is a diagnosis of the human condition.

The original command was given to Adam before Eve was created. This detail matters. When we later read the exchange between Eve and the Serpent, we witness how interpretation quietly intrudes, fracturing the wholeness of reality. The dialogue reveals how truth, once received, becomes vulnerable the moment it is edited.

The Serpent begins not with denial, but with distortion: *"Did God really say, 'You must not eat from any tree in the garden?'"* (Genesis 3:1 (NIV)

The question is subtle, almost innocent, yet its purpose is surgical — to loosen trust.

"God did say, "You must not eat fruit from the tree that is in the middle of the garden, and you must not touch it, or you will die." "" (Genesis 3:2–3(NIV)

When Eve responds, she does not simply repeat God's command. She adds to it: *"You must not touch it."* That instruction was never given by God.

Whether this addition originated with Eve or was inherited through Adam, the effect is the same: God's word is no longer received as given but filtered through human reasoning, which now stands beside God's word instead of beneath it. And this is the first step toward assuming God's role.

The Serpent then advances the deception further — not only undermining God's authority, but casting doubt on His goodness. "You will not certainly die, the serpent said to the woman." God is portrayed as either fearful or withholding, guarding power rather than sharing love. And then comes the promise the Serpent cannot fulfill: *You will be like God, knowing good and evil.* (Genesis 3:4–5 (NIV)

This moment is often misunderstood. The temptation is not knowledge itself. It is authority.

Who decides what is good?

Who defines what is evil?

Who names reality?

Genesis 3 is the moment humanity declares: *I will decide.*

"Then the eyes of both of them were opened…" (Genesis 3:7 (NIV)

But what did they see?

Not God.

Not truth.

Not wisdom.

They saw *themselves.*

Self-consciousness replaced God-consciousness. Shame replaced innocence. Covering replaced trust. This was the birth of identity confusion.

Immediately, unity fractured. Adam blamed Eve. Eve blamed the serpent. Relationships have turned adversarial. Even God was subtly implicated:

*"The woman **You** put here with me…"* (Genesis 3:12)

This is the first us *versus them.*

In Genesis 3:16, God says: "I will greatly increase your pains in childbearing."

And here lies the paradox.

The first human pain after Eden is not execution. God does not respond to betrayal with extinction. He responds with birth.

Pain does not end the story. Pain becomes the pathway through which the story continues. Not punishment, but boundary. A reminder humanity desperately needed:

You are not God.

Here is where our focus often stops. Conditioned by culture to rely on self-constructed truth, we cling to a familiar accusation: *We disobeyed, and God inflicted pain.* Yet this claim is another refusal of responsibility. We shift the burden back onto God and ask the same questions generation after generation:

Why would He deny us knowledge?

Why allow deception?

If He created everything, why create evil?

Scripture answers with uncomfortable clarity.

God did not deny knowledge — He denied *premature authority.*

God did not create evil — evil is not a substance, but the absence of God.

And deception was permitted because love without choice is coercion, not love.

Knowledge without relationship produces domination. Knowledge received within relationship produces wisdom.

And here we forget a crucial truth: humanity was never forbidden to eat from the *Tree of Life.*

Life was offered freely.

But life was not enough.

We chose instead the fruit that promised elevation — to sit on the throne, to name good and evil for ourselves. We wanted authority, not communion. And so, we were reminded of who we are: clay.

This was not cruelty.

It was mercy restraining self-destruction.

What would you choose today, if offered the same decision? Knowledge — or life?

For me, the answer is clear. I chose life. Because life with God ultimately brings knowledge. God does not withhold truth. God is truth. God is knowledge.

What we so often miss in the story of our creation is this: humanity introduced pain into a perfect world. Pain entered history not as punishment, but as betrayal.

The tragedy of Eden is not that humanity desired to know — but that we chose knowing over being known, understanding over relationship, mastery over trust.

And in doing so, we wounded God.

That truth is rarely spoken plainly. Betrayal caused God pain — real, relational pain. The God who formed humanity from dust and breath, who walked with them in the cool of the day, who entrusted them with creation, was rejected. His voice doubted. His goodness questioned. His presence, treated as insufficient.

And here lies the paradox that defines the entire biblical narrative: God does not retaliate against pain. He transforms it.

The first transformation happens immediately. God does not erase the wound; He reassigns its meaning. Pain becomes a signal — a warning light on the dashboard of the soul. Not condemnation, but communication. Not punishment, but invitation.

Pain begins to say: *Something is wrong. You are separated from life.*

Later, God transforms pain again — not merely into signal, but into redemption. He does not remove suffering from the human story; He enters it. He carries it. He redeems it from the inside.

And finally, pain is transformed a third time — into transcendence. What once marked separation becomes the place of reunion. What once signaled death becomes the passage into life.

Pain entered history as broken trust, and every later pain is an echo of this first wound.

This is the arc from Eden to Golgotha: pain begins as rupture, pain becomes message, pain is redeemed, pain is transfigured.

The forbidden fruit promised knowledge of good and evil. The Tree of Life promised God.

And humanity chose poorly.

Yet even then — even after betrayal — God did not withdraw life. He preserved it, until humanity would be ready to receive it again — not by grasping, but by surrender.

The final invitation of Scripture is not to knowledge, but to life:

"Whoever believes in Me shall live." (John 11:25–26)

The Tree of Life was never forbidden.

It was always waiting.

And it still is.

CHAPTER 12

The Mirrors and Faces of Pain

The Fall happens in a moment.
The descent takes generations.

Mirror, mirror on the wall......

After the rupture in Eden, humanity does not heal — it adapts. It learns to live with separation: by denying pain, by using it, enforcing it, and by erasing those who carry it. Until it forgets how to feel at all.

From this lens, history is not a straight line. It is a cathedral built of mirrors — each unveiled not by chronology, but by conscience. They turn slowly, one by one, until the faces they reflect begin to look uncomfortably like our own.

***

Mirror I — Containment

Pain that is contained rather than confessed does not heal — it metastasizes.

Between 1993 and 1994, Bulgaria entered a period of severe economic collapse. Regional instability, including the UN embargo against Serbia and Montenegro, severed key trade routes and disrupted energy supplies. The disintegration of Soviet-era economic systems compounded the damage. Inflation surged. The lev[6] collapsed. Real wages fell by more than fourteen percent in 1994 alone. By 1996, the country descended into hyperinflation.

My sons were four and three years old.

I was working as an investigative reporter for one of the first private

6. the Bulgarian currency

television stations in Burgas. In January 1996, my monthly salary was 9,000 leva — about $128. By October, it had risen to 12,000 leva — worth only $52.

At the same time, prices exploded.

My boys' favorite cookies, **Zakuska** — the ones they loved crumbled into yogurt — became my quiet unit of measurement. In 1994, one package cost 30 leva: roughly 0.3% of my monthly income. By 1996, the same cookies cost 1,000 leva — over 8% of my salary. Nothing about the cookies had changed. Everything else had.

That was the moment I decided to begin court proceedings against Boris for child support. I believed — naively — that justice might lessen the strain.

Instead, it multiplied the pain.

Boris arrived at court with Lily. The judge ordered him to pay 3,000 leva per month for both children — the equivalent of three packages of Zakuska cookies. I stood there as Boris and Lily whispered to his attorney, who then appealed the court's decision.

The humiliation was quiet. Surgical. Precise.

I lifted my chin.

I walked away and never looked back.

And I contained my pain.

That instinct — to deny pain in order to survive — is not a personal failure. It is a learned human reflex. And when pain is contained long enough, it does not disappear. It relocates. It hardens. It spreads.

This is how collective pain begins.

***

On the night of April 24, 1915, the Ottoman capital of Constantinople did not fall asleep.

Under orders issued by the Minister of the Interior, Talaat Pasha, soldiers moved through the city with lists in their hands. They came to silence the voices of the elite. Two hundred and seventy Armenian leaders were arrested in a single night — poets and physicians, lawyers and musicians, editors, parliamentarians — the thinkers, healers, and memory-keepers of the people. By morning, the head had been severed from the body — in a very literal sense, too.

April 24 would later be called *Red Sunday.* History would mark it as the beginning of the Armenian Genocide. But for those who lived it, it was the moment pain crossed a threshold — from violence into erasure.

What followed was methodical.

Families vanished from villages that had spoken their names for centuries. Churches burned until prayer had no walls left to echo within. Languages were buried alongside bodies, as if words themselves could be erased. People were not merely killed — they were removed.

One and a half million Armenians were systematically exterminated.

And then, almost immediately, the second wound opened.

Silence.

What could not be denied outright was neutralized. What could not be erased physically was managed politically. Memory was pushed into footnotes. Grief was fenced off by treaties. Diplomacy put on the garments of peace while refusing the garment of repentance.

This is the cold logic of containment: the facts are not denied — they are recognized and *finished.* Recorded in archives but withheld from the human heart. Pain is commemorated, managed, controlled.

Containment does not erase pain. It preserves it — untreated, silent, alone. And pain preserved becomes inheritance: shaping identity, distorting trust, breeding bitterness where healing was denied.

The Armenian Genocide is not the only face reflected in this mirror.

The Trail of Tears bears the same shape. Treaties were signed. Apologies were spoken. Textbooks were written. And yet the land still remembers. Descendants still carry grief that was acknowledged but never redeemed. Cultures were declared "past" while their pain was declared "over."

The mirror of containment confronts us with an uncomfortable truth: history can be acknowledged and still remain unresolved, because healing requires more than memory.

Pain not redeemed does not disappear — it is repurposed.

Grief becomes leverage.

Suffering becomes currency.

Human bodies become means.

And thus, history steps from containment into its next distortion — and *the mirror turns.*

Mirror II — Exploitation

Imagine a cluster of islands scattered across the western White Sea, less than a hundred miles from the Arctic Circle — a place where the world feels unfinished, still breathing its first breath. Granite and gneiss rise in uneven hills. Wind-swept tundra yields to forests of Scots pine and Norway spruce. Hundreds of glacial lakes — three hundred, perhaps five hundred — lie calm as glass, many connected by ancient canals carved five centuries ago by monks who believed water could teach patience.

Winter here is long. Dark. Absolute.

For most of the year, the sea is locked in ice, navigation possible only for a few fragile summer months. Northern winds howl without obstruction. The White Sea crashes against stone shores while, in the distance, beluga whales churn the water into a strange, boiling song — primeval, haunting, beautiful.

At the center of this frozen archipelago stands a fortress.

The *Solovetsky Monastery*[7] rises behind walls eight to eleven meters high — stone thick enough to defy time, faith, and artillery. Once a sanctuary of prayer and silence, it became something else entirely: the prototype. The experiment. The mother of the Gulag[8].

Beauty did not protect this place from evil.

Instead, it hid it in plain sight.

Where monks once prayed, prisoners were cataloged. Where bells once called men to worship, boots marched them to punishment. Pain was no longer consequence. It became method.

To extract obedience.

To erase individuality.

To turn human beings into instruments — expendable, replaceable, silent.

On Mount Sekirnaya — crowned with a cathedral and a staircase of 365 stone steps — the camp's "criminal department" operated with

7. Dmitry Likhachev, a young scholar imprisoned there, wrote of how Solovetsky transformed from a place of intellectual exile into something far darker — a laboratory where guards executed prisoners for minor infractions, simply to reinforce authority.

8. Aleksandr Solzhenitsyn named Solovetsky what it was: the mother of the Gulag, in his book The Gulag Archipelago

chilling precision. Prisoners were tied to heavy logs and rolled down the staircase. Bodies tumbled. Bones broke. Lives ended at the foot of a holy hill. The steps still stand.

Elsewhere, punishment known as "On Mosquitoes"[9] awaited those who displeased their guards. Naked prisoners were bound to trees for hours — sometimes overnight — in clouds of insects so dense the air seemed alive. Bodies swelled. Skin split. Some died not from wounds, but from shock — pain too total to endure.

Others were forced into the White Sea in late autumn, standing neck-deep in freezing water or dragging waterlogged logs to shore with bare hands[10]. Some were left outside in winter, positioned deliberately so survival was impossible, until frost finished what cruelty began.

Scripture names this crime without euphemism:

"Look! The wages you failed to pay the workers who mowed your fields are crying out against you. The cries of the harvesters have reached the ears of the Lord Almighty." (James 5:4)

***

This is how exploitation works: through structure.

Pain is measured, applied, repeated — until suffering becomes commodified, instrumentalized, capitalized upon.

And here is the lie that comforts us: that such brutality belongs only to regimes, camps, uniforms, distant histories.

It does not.

The state only perfects what the human heart is already willing to practice. A camp is intimacy scaled up — power discovering that another person's pain can be used.

I learned that in my own home.

The man I loved — the father of my children — once held me over the balcony of our third-floor apartment in Burgas. He was angry. I had asked him to leave the illegal activities I suspected. I had asked him to return to us — to his sons — to be the father they needed.

We argued.

Yes, I was yelling.

---

9. Oleg Volkov, in Diving into Darkness, described the mosquito torture as "sophisticated," not in method but in intention — pain calibrated, prolonged, observed.

10. B. Sederkholm documented the agony of the White Sea punishments — the way cold penetrated not the skin, but the will.

I was screaming my pain aloud.

Pain can make us visible. And visibility can be dangerous.

A month later, another fight followed me into the market. He shouted. Called me names. Pushed the stroller so violently, my infant son lifted into the air. I fled home. He followed. The argument escalated.

Then — light.

Then darkness.

I remember my sons crying somewhere far away, as if underwater.

I lay on the floor. Eyes swollen. Chest hollow. My cheekbone shattered — the cracking sound replaying for nights afterward. The cold, metallic taste of blood in my mouth.

My longing for love.

My hope for reconciliation.

My fear of being alone.

All of it became his license to control. No uniform was required. No ideology had to be written. He needed only proximity, power, and the decision to cross a line.

In the Gulag, pain was industrialized.

In my life, it was intimate.

***

The goal is always the same: to objectify pain.

When pain becomes a thing — something to be managed, minimized, endured — it no longer demands response; it only requires efficiency.

History performs the same operation at scale. In systems like the Gulag, suffering is analyzed, categorized, absorbed into "objective" frameworks. Individual lives dissolve into data. Personal histories flatten into case studies. Human wounds are repurposed for collective narratives.

What is lost is not information — but dignity. Pain that is objectified ceases to be a moral claim. No one is responsible. No one needs to repent.

***

The mirror blinks.

The image shifts — vast ocean, a ship on the horizon.

Endless blue waters. Wind in the sails. Sunlight flashing across the surface. From afar, it looks like freedom. Almost like hope.

Then you step below deck.

The air collapses around you — thick, sour, unbreathable. Bodies stacked tighter than cargo, chained ankle to ankle, wrist to wrist, pressed into wooden shelves slick with sweat, blood, vomit, and waste. No room to turn. No room to sit. No room to die properly. Disease spreads faster than speech — dysentery, smallpox, fever. The groans do not stop.

Children cry until their voices disappear. Mothers go silent before their babies do. Some are thrown overboard still breathing.

Efficiency.

The sea closes over them without protest.

Ship after ship.

It was a hungry industry.

The transatlantic slave trade was engineered by order. Ships were measured. Human bodies counted. Losses calculated in profit margins. Pain reduced to the cost of doing business.

And here the pattern clarifies: power, untethered from accountability, always finds language to justify cruelty.

Those who stood on deck — educated, baptized, civilized — did not see themselves as monsters. They spoke of commerce. Destiny. Progress. Even God's will. Language functioned like chains: restraining conscience.

This is how exploitation works.

It does not begin with hatred.

It begins with distance.

Distance between "us" and "them."

Between action and consequence.

Between profit and blood.

When people are reduced to labor, when suffering becomes currency, when bodies become tools — evil no longer needs rage to survive. It only needs permission.

And here the accusation turns upward.

How do we speak of God in a world where His name was invoked above decks slick with human misery? How do we read Scripture where slavery appears within its pages? Does God sanctify domination — or expose it?

These questions cannot be dismissed. Nor answered cheaply[11]. Because what is at stake is not only history — but truth itself.

Whether God stands with power — or stands against it. Whether Scripture reflects cruelty — or interrupts it.

Before we answer, we must look honestly at the mirror.

Exploitation did not end with chains.

It only learned to change its shape.

And so, the mirror turns.

Mirror III — Domination and the Authority to Erase

"Now the earth was corrupt in God's sight,
and the earth was filled with violence." (Genesis 6:11)

I was not born into cruelty — I learned it.

When we returned from Libya in 1985, I was seventeen — restless, hungry for belonging, utterly unanchored. The Revival Process[12] had already begun. Nationalist fervor filled the streets like oxygen — protests, chants, slogans, demands.

Only Bulgarian language.

Only Bulgarian names.

Only Bulgarian identity.

History had been simplified for us, sharpened into a weapon. We were taught that we had been slaves for five hundred years under Ottoman rule — a distortion repeated so often it felt like truth. There was suffering, yes. Blood. Resistance. Loss. But we were not slaves.

That distortion mattered. It prepared us to justify what came next.

At eighteen, I was not a bystander. I was an activist. I spoke publicly.

11. Because the question of slavery — and the accusation that God condones it — requires careful distinction rather than reaction, it will be addressed fully in the Appendix Q&A, where history and Scripture can be examined without distortion

12. The "Revival Process" (Bulgarian: Vazroditelen protses) was a brutal campaign of forced assimilation conducted by Bulgaria's communist government between 1984 and 1989.

I invoked Hristo Botev:

"Tell me, tell me, poor nation —
who rocks you in this cradle of slavery?"[13]

And I felt righteous as the words left my mouth.

I believed I was defending freedom.

I was not.

I was calling for the erasure of other human beings — their names, their language, their memory — and I did it without hatred in my heart. That is the most terrifying part.

I was not defending Christianity.

I was disguising arrogance as patriotism.

Violence as justice.

Collective sin as historical correction.

Looking back now, this is one of the deepest shames of my life — not because I was evil, but because I was convinced, I was good.

This is what ideology does when God is absent: it teaches you to confuse righteousness with dominance and belonging with obedience.

I did not need to be forced.

I volunteered.

***

What followed was not an accident of history, but a systematic assault on identity.

The Revival Process stands as one of the most shameful chapters in Bulgaria's modern past. A nation that had resisted Nazi pressure during World War II — saving approximately 48,000 to 50,000 Bulgarian Jews from deportation in 1943 — turned, four decades later, against its own citizens.

Under the false premise that ethnic Turks were "originally Bulgarian," forcibly converted during Ottoman rule, the state moved to erase difference.

Between 850,000 and 1.3 million people were compelled to replace their Turkish and Arabic names with Slavic ones chosen from government lists. The Turkish language was banned in public. Islamic rituals

13. Hristo Botev (1848–1876), from the poem "Моята молитва" ("My Prayer"), 1875. English translation by the author, based on the original Bulgarian text. This line was widely taught and invoked in Bulgarian nationalist discourse to frame the Ottoman period as one of total enslavement — a simplification that later contributed to ideological misuse of history.

were criminalized. Traditional clothing was prohibited. Male circumcision was outlawed.

Resistance was crushed. Villages were surrounded by troops and tanks. Thousands were beaten, imprisoned, or sent to the Belene labor camp. Conservative estimates place the dead between 800 and 2,500.

In 1989, the border with Turkey was opened, triggering the forced exodus of more than 360,000 people. The regime called it "voluntary migration."

History calls it what it was: ethnic cleansing.

"Woe to those who make unjust laws, to those who issue oppressive decrees… to deprive the poor of their rights and withhold justice from the oppressed." (Isaiah 10:1–2)

***

What the Revival Process reveals is not an anomaly, but a mechanism.

Domination does not begin with violence.

It begins with definition.

With classification.

With calculation.

Forced renaming is not the opposite of genocide — it is its rehearsal. When difference is framed as disorder and unity is enforced rather than received, power no longer needs hatred to function.

It only needs compliance.

The Kurdish experience follows this same architecture of domination, carried to its logical extreme. When identity is treated as a threat to order, the body eventually becomes expendable. When ideology replaces moral restraint, destruction can be planned with bureaucratic calm, scientific precision, and administrative justification.

The tools may vary.

The doctrine does not:

"I decide."

God has always rejected atrocities committed "in His name."

"They have built the high places… to burn their sons and their daugh-

ters in the fire, which I did not command, nor did it come into My mind." (Jeremiah 7:31)

Erasing pain by erasing people is the final rebellion.

Halabja was part of the Anfal campaign — politically driven yet cloaked in religious rhetoric. The Iraqi regime invoked "Anfal" — the eighth chapter of the Qur'an, meaning "spoils of war" — to sanctify its campaign against the Kurds.

Once again, humanity assumed the authority to define good and evil, life and death, without reference to God.

***

In a lush valley, 700 to 900 meters above sea level, in the Shahrizor plain at the base of the Zagros Mountains, lies the "City of Poets" — Halabja.

On March 16, 1988, shortly before Newroz — the Kurdish New Year — the city was alive with the colors of early spring and the quiet anticipation of celebration. The cross-shaped streets, laid out by French engineers in 1933, were filled with laughter and the scent of freshly baked bread.

It was a beautiful day.

Around 11 a.m., that garden-like city was methodically redesigned into ruin.

Iraqi jets and artillery pounded Halabja with conventional explosives, rockets, and napalm. This was not random destruction — it was preparation. The bombardment shattered windows and doors, driving civilians into underground cellars and air-raid shelters.

Spaces that would soon become traps.

Thirty-five minutes later, the second phase began.

Omar Khawar, a 34-year-old gardener and father of eight daughters and twin sons, was at home when the bombing started. In a desperate, split-second decision, he sent his family toward the mountains, hoping they might reach safety across the Iranian border, ten to fifteen kilometers away.

Then came the smell.

Almost like a peace offering.

Sweet.

Familiar.

Apples.

The lethal mixture — sarin, mustard gas, hydrogen cyanide, tabun — seeped through shattered windows, broken ventilation pipes, basement stairwells. Because these gases were heavier than air, they sank downward, pooling in the shelters where families had fled.

The sweetness drew some out — especially children — toward windows and streets where the concentration was strongest.

Photographs from that day show the sky transformed into a kaleidoscope of poison — white, yellow, greenish, black — rolling slowly through the streets, collapsing the boundary between earth and air.

The city suffocated under its own sky.

In the chaos, Omar was separated from his family. He was found later clutching one infant — Mohammed.

Neither survived.

It was later confirmed that Omar's wife and all eight of his daughters were killed in the attack. Omar died twenty meters from his front door; his face wrapped in a jamadani — a traditional Kurdish scarf — in a futile attempt to filter the air. His body shielded the child until the end.

Halabja was not a deviation from history.

It was its consequence.

An estimated 5,000 people were killed in a matter of hours. In a single day.

"They shed innocent blood…

and the land was polluted with blood." (Psalm 106:38)

Pain, when wielded by human hands, becomes strategic.

It is no longer accidental.

It is calculated.

Measured.

Timed.

Justified.

Domination begins with definition.

It matures into erasure.

And it culminates in the authority to decide who may breathe.
Eden echoes through history — humanity grasping the throne.
And the mirror turns.

Mirror IV — Weaponized Memory

(The fracture that follows)

What happened in Halabja was not an act of God.

God does not design gas chambers, authorize chemical clouds, or script the suffocation of children. He does not require cruelty to accomplish His purposes, nor does He sanctify violence carried out in His name. Scripture does not deny judgment or suffering — but it distinguishes them from evil. Divine judgment belongs to God alone; it is never delegated to human domination.

Evil enters when people assume authority they were never given and clothe it in necessity, ideology, or righteousness.

"Why does God allow this?" many ask.

He does not approve of it. But He grants freedom — and love that revokes freedom becomes tyranny. A world without choice might be orderly, but it would not be good. And so, God permits what He hates, grieves what He allows, and judges what humanity insists on doing despite His word.

Every system that claims the right to decide who may live and who must disappear is a false god made operational. It may speak the language of security, purity, progress, or historical necessity, but it is born from the same ancient rupture — the moment humanity chose to define good and evil apart from its Creator.

God does not orchestrate such choices. He permits them, confronts them, and ultimately redeems what they destroy. But the hand that drops the gas is human — not divine.

Yet domination is not the final fracture.

After the killing ends, something more subtle begins.

Memory.

***

Pain does not end when violence stops.

It settles.

It waits.

And when it is neither confessed nor redeemed, it hardens into inheritance.

Memory becomes the vessel through which suffering changes form and is carried forward as identity.

Unresolved pain becomes story.

Story becomes self-definition.

Self-definition becomes permission.

When memory is weaponized, the past is no longer remembered to be healed — it is remembered to justify the next wound. Trauma becomes sacred property. Grief becomes moral capital. History ceases to teach and begins to shield.

This is the fracture that follows domination.

Rwanda stands as one of the clearest demonstrations of this transformation.

The 1994 genocide against the Tutsi did not erupt from ancient hatred alone. It was engineered through the weaponization of historical trauma. Colonial rule had already hardened fluid identities into racial categories, embedding grievance into bureaucracy through identity cards and hierarchy. Political elites later harvested this inherited pain and reshaped it into ideology.

Through hate media such as Radio Télévision Libre des Mille Collines, memory was rehearsed, narrated, ritualized — until suffering itself became lethal. Tutsis were framed not as neighbors, but as an existential threat: past, present, and future.

When the killing began, neighbors did not suddenly become monsters. They became executors of a story they had been taught to inhabit — a story where survival required elimination.

Pain was not denied.

It was preserved.

And then unleashed.

Even the end of the genocide did not end the cycle. The victory of the Rwandan Patriotic Front stopped the massacre, but fear reproduced itself in another direction. Nearly two million Hutus fled into neighboring countries, terrified of reprisal. Trauma simply changed hands. Memory did not heal.

It migrated.

To prevent another descent into violence, Rwanda attempted something extraordinary: restorative justice through the Gacaca courts. Justice was brought out of distant institutions and into village squares. Perpetrators confessed before survivors. Truth was spoken face to face. In places like the Mbyo Reconciliation Village, former killers and victims' families now farm the same land — a fragile testament to what radical truth-telling can achieve.

Pain, confronted directly, lost some of its power to reproduce itself. And yet peace came at a cost. For many survivors, forgiveness was mandated faster than healing could occur. Studies decades later reveal that nearly one-third still suffer severe PTSD, often intensified by public testimony. Silence under the banner of reconciliation risks becoming another burial — a wound dressed lightly before it has closed.

Scripture warns of this danger:

"They dress the wound of my people as though it were not serious.

'Peace, peace, 'they say, when there is no peace." (Jeremiah 8:11)

Peace declared too early can become another kind of violence.

The opposite danger appears when pain is not suppressed — but amplified.

After September 11, 2001, grief in the United States was real, deep, and undeniable. But when memory ceased to be mourning and became a permanent state of emergency, pain crossed a threshold. Trauma hardened into identity. Identity became moral permission.

History was no longer remembered to be healed — it was invoked to justify what followed. Policies were framed not as choices, but as obligations to the dead. Violence was defended not as strategy, but as memory's demand.

The pain was not processed.

It was exported.

"See to it that no bitter root grows up to cause trouble and defile many." (Hebrews 12:15)

When grief is nursed rather than transformed, it does not remain private. It spreads. It teaches the next wound how to arrive already justified.

***

A Mother's Confession

I saw this mechanism not only in nations — but in myself.

When the man I loved, Boris, was taken from me, my grief did not disappear. I nursed it. I let it define me. And because I did not yet know how to surrender it, it began to spread.

My grief spiraled into a desperate search for love through lust — a polygamy of the soul — where I tried to fill an infinite void with fleeting connections. I filled my days to avoid my nights. I convinced myself I was unlovable unless I was wanted. I sealed my heart with work, study, and hollow relationships — and in doing so, I starved my sons of the mother I longed to be.

To my sons: this is my public apology.

I am deeply sorry for the light I let grow dim.

Pain taught me how to injure what I feared losing. I mistook wounds for identity and bitterness for strength. Setbacks became verdicts. Grief became self-sabotage.

This fracture followed me into my work. I served as a domestic violence investigator — a role I loved and excelled in. When I was passed over for promotion and later reprimanded under circumstances that felt unjust, I did not respond with clarity. I interpreted it not as a painful professional setback, but as confirmation of my deepest fear: that I was expendable.

Instead of facing loss, I fled — resigning, uprooting my life, returning to Bulgaria not in discernment but retreat. I kept falling under the weight of untransformed pain until God began teaching me — slowly — how fear can become peace and surrender can become grace.

When I returned to the United States after more than three years away, my family was shattered. One son was fighting for his children through courts and accusations. The other had just welcomed a new child while still grieving the loss of his first.

Words spoken in pain became weapons. Brothers stood divided by wounds they could not name. Everyone felt betrayed. Everyone believed they were right.

No one was whole.

Pain spread like cancer — justifying itself at every step.

When my younger son opened his heart to God in the midst of that fracture, the distance between us felt wider. I did not yet understand that God was not dividing us — He was offering escape from the cycle.

It took a year of wrestling and surrender for me to see: the same Lord who met my son was reaching for me. Without Him, I would have lost not only arguments — but relationships.

Not because love was absent.

But because darkness was suffocating it.

***

What happens in families happens in nations — only with flags, borders, and children who inherit wounds they did not choose.

The conflict between Israel and Gaza reflects this same architecture of weaponized memory. Trauma is inherited. On one side, the Holocaust becomes a lens through which every threat is existential. On the other, the Nakba remains an unbroken present, confirming that survival requires perpetual resistance.

Each side remembers — not to heal, but to prove necessity.

Children grow up inside these memories before they can question them. Grief becomes curriculum. Fear and pain become identity. And peace feels like betrayal. Restraint - like weakness. The enemy must remain monstrous — or the story collapses.

Scripture does not excuse either extreme.

"Do not seek revenge or bear a grudge," the Law commands (Leviticus 19:18) — not because justice is irrelevant, but because hatred metastasizes.

And yet God also rebukes false peace that refuses to name the wound. The biblical path is narrow and difficult:

Truth without vengeance.

Memory without hatred.

Justice without eradication.

Memory itself is not evil. Remembering is sacred. But when memory becomes authority — when it decides who may live and who must disappear — it becomes a false god.

When pain is neither surrendered nor transformed, it reproduces itself with precision.

The most dangerous illusion is that remembering pain will heal it. God does not ask us to forget. He asks us to remember rightly — in a way that leads to repentance, restraint, and reconciliation. Because memory, when redeemed, becomes testimony. Memory, when weaponized, becomes destiny.

And so, the mirror turns again.

Mirror V — Anesthesia

After domination, after erasure, after vengeance has exhausted itself, something quieter arrives.

Numbness.

This is not peace.

It is the absence of pain without the presence of healing.

The world does not stop hurting.

We simply stop feeling.

Pain — once contained, then exploited, then weaponized — becomes too heavy to carry. And so, humanity invents anesthesia. Not to cure the wound, but to silence it. Not to restore meaning, but to dull sensation.

The ache remains.

It is simply padded, distracted, sedated.

Digital glow replaces reflection. Screens flicker where silence once lived. Endless scrolling becomes a refuge from stillness — because stillness remembers. Algorithms learn our wounds and feed us comfort on demand: entertainment, outrage, validation, escape — anything but presence.

The mental health crisis is not mysterious. It is the predictable consequence of unresolved pain in a world that refuses to pause long enough to name it. Anxiety. Depression. Dissociation. These are not moral failures. They are signals from a soul asked to endure without meaning and survive without hope.

Comfort culture promises relief but delivers amnesia.

Self-soothe.

Self-optimize.

Self-medicate.

Self-define.

Anything but surrender.

We curate wellness while avoiding truth. We anesthetize grief with pleasure and call it freedom.

This mirror does not rage.

It does not protest.

It quietly binds us with invisible chains, engulfing us into our reflections. And the chant echoes:

Mirror, mirror on the wall. . . .

Now the arc becomes visible:

Containment taught us to silence pain.

Exploitation taught us to trade it.

Domination taught us to wield it.

Erasure taught us to deny it.

Vengeance taught us to multiply it.

Anesthesia teaches us to forget it.

This is the architecture of fallen humanity.

But numbness is not the end.

The body remembers what the mind suppresses. The soul resists being reduced to circuitry and sedation. Beneath distraction, something still aches — not for comfort, but for meaning. Not for escape, but for restoration.

Here the paradox returns:

Pain unfelt becomes despair.

Pain faced, becomes transformation.

This mirror closes not with horror, but with a question:

What if the opposite of numbness is not suffering — but truth? What if feeling again is not a threat — but a way home?

This is not the end of the story.

It is the moment the anesthesia begins to wear off.

And we breathe again.

***

There was a time when I could no longer feel my own life.

Muted. Lonely. Unseen.

Misunderstood. Unnecessary.

I was not looking for spectacle. I was starving for relief.

So, I booked a trip to Ecuador.

The ceremony at Gaia Sagrada begins with a threshold. As the sun sinks behind the Andes, two "Guards of the Gate" stand at the entrance of the maloca[14] — sober sentinels anchoring the physical world while others prepare to slip beneath its surface. To pass them is to leave ordinary reality and enter ritual space.

Inside, darkness gathers around a central fire. The shaman's assistant shapes glowing embers into what they call the Fire Bird — a phoenix-like figure of living flame. It becomes symbol, witness, guide.

The Icaros rise — medicine songs weaving through the air. Participants wait for the brew to take hold.

Heat does not consume, they say. It refines.

In that space, grief is invited to surface.

Then comes what they call the *Ceremony of Truth.* One by one, we are summoned forward to sit before the embers. Masks fall. Stories surface.

When my turn came, the heat brushed my face like a demand for honesty. The medicine peeled back layers of what I once called my "polygamy of the soul" — my desperate search for love in a thousand empty places — until I saw the root beneath it.

I was there to forgive.

14. a traditional, large, communal longhouse of various Indigenous peoples in the Amazon rainforest. It serves as a central hub for daily life, social gatherings, and spiritual ceremonies, housing multiple families together under one roof.

I spoke my father's name.

I spoke of physical and psychological abuse. Of abandonment. Of years without a mother. Of loneliness so deep it became identity. Of anxiety. Of night terrors that paralyzed me — unable to move, unable to scream.

I spoke because my voice had long been buried.

The shaman listened and named what she perceived: a spiritual assault — an infernal battle for my soul. She prepared a ritual of symbolic transference, declaring that what tormented me must be sent back to the fire.

And then something unexpected happened.

She invoked the name of Jesus.

She told the circle that when evil is encountered, Jesus is the highest authority[15].

I was stunned.

I knew the ceremony was not Christian. I knew fire was being treated as mediator. Yet the Name pierced through the confusion with unmistakable clarity.

In that moment, something shifted — not because of the ritual, but because of Him.

When I returned to my mat, I felt lighter. The night terrors stopped. They have never returned.

Looking back now with the light of the Lord in my heart, I see the terrifying and beautiful complexity of that night. I had fallen into the enemy's trap — looking for help in a place where the Creator was substituted for the creature, where God was exchanged for the Fire. And yet His love is so relentless that He did not abandon me to that mistake.

He entered it.

He reached into a place He does not sanctify to rescue someone He refused to lose.

He left the ninety-nine.[16]

He stepped into the swamp.

He reached into the pit of my darkness.[17]

Not to endorse the altar — but to reclaim the offering.

Me!

---

15. Philippians 2:9-10: "...the name that is above every name, that at the name of Jesus every knee should bow." (Supporting the Shaman's claim of His Power).

16. Luke 15:4: "Doesn't he leave the ninety-nine in the open country and go after the lost sheep until he finds it?"

17. Psalm 139:8: "If I make my bed in the depths, you are there." (Confirming that He entered the "swamp" to find you).

***

Once again, God showed me immense mercy and patience.

I see it now: God was already breathing life into me long before I knew His name. Long before I understood His Gospel. Long before I could surrender fully. He was there — holding my hand in the fire so I would not be alone.

The anesthesia wears off, numbness breaks and space for truth is made.

No, the pain is not gone — but it is finally seen for what it is – a transformative power.

CHAPTER 13

El-Roi, the God Who Sees

Not long ago in church, I heard a song by Hillsong United and Taya. One line lingered long after the music ended:

"There is another in the fire, standing next to me."

Every time I hear it now, I see wildfire.

It begins small. Flickering.

And I am standing in the middle of it.

I tell myself it will pass. I remain where I am. The space around me narrows slowly enough that I convince myself I am still safe. The flames rise higher, licking at the walls of what I once believed was solid ground. The air burns my lungs, but I keep breathing — shallow, careful breaths — afraid that anything deeper might undo me.

I endure the heat.

My skin stings. Then blisters. Pain sharpens, becomes constant, and I learn to live inside it. I call this courage. I call it strength. I call it perseverance.

I look for exits. Every direction glow red.

Still, I do not move.

Because somewhere inside, I believe needing help is failure. That surrender is a collapse.

But the fire does not recede.

It grows.

Violent. Alive. Consuming the last illusion of distance between me and destruction.

And then the truth arrives — clear and merciless: If I stay here, I will be consumed. This is the moment I understand: I cannot do this alone.

I finally look. And I see His hand stretched toward me — not dragging me out, not forcing rescue — but waiting.

God has never left the fire.

He has been there the entire time.

Waiting for me to choose Him.

Waiting for me to take His hand.
Even there.
Even in Gaia Sagrada.

***

Millennia before my own fire, there was a woman named Hagar. She was a shadow in another person's story; a displaced Egyptian used as a vessel for a promise she didn't ask to carry. But she fell into the trap of human pride and the vicious circle of mistreatment and resentment started spinning. When the heat of Sarah's contempt became wildfire, Hagar did what I have so often done: she fled. She ran until the air turned to dust and the horizon offered nothing but silence.

Standing by a desert spring, broken and invisible to the world that had discarded her, she discovered the same mercy I found in the flames. She didn't find a God who simply watched from a distance; she found a God who was already there, waiting in the wilderness.

In that moment of total exposure, she did something no prophet or patriarch had done before: she gave God a name. She called Him El-Roi. *The God Who Sees Me.*

She realized that being seen by God is the beginning of being saved by God. But the revelation carries a weight—a question that bridges the desert of Genesis to the streets of modern-day Harlem.

***

Recently I watched the Netflix series based on true events *When They See Us* — the story of five boys from Harlem who were falsely accused, condemned, and imprisoned for a crime they did not commit.

Many watching that story ask the same questions:

Where was God? Why did He not intervene sooner? Why did He not expose the lie immediately? Why did He allow their suffering at all?

To some, such injustice appears to prove His absence. But absence is not the same as silence. And silence is not the same as indifference.

God does not design injustice to produce character.

Evil is not His instrument.

But He refuses to abandon those who suffer under it.

Those young men walked through years of humiliation and loss. That was wrong. It was the product of human arrogance, racial prejudice, and institutional failure. Yet even in that wrong, God did not withdraw. He sustained them. He preserved their sanity. He guarded what the system tried to erase.

It is easy to believe that a loving God would never allow such things to happen. But love, real love, is not indulgent; it is redemptive. Love allows us to walk through the valley not to punish us, but to teach us that the valley does not own us.

God's justice often moves slower than our pain, but it moves perfectly. When His work is finished, the broken become healers, the victims become witnesses, and the story that once felt like proof of His absence becomes evidence of His presence. For even in the darkest prisons, God's eyes never close. He does not see us as the world does — guilty, broken, lost — but as His children, still forming under His patient hand.

He is the Potter; we are the clay. (Isaiah 64:8 (NIV) And even when the clay is pressed and cracked, the Potter's hands never leave it.

Those boys walked through prejudice and discrimination, but they came out as living parables of grace. Their stories remind me that faith is not proven by what we avoid, but by what we endure. When we allow God to turn our pain into purpose, He shows us that even injustice can become the birthplace of redemption.

Because our God is not only the One who reigns above suffering — He is **the God who sees.**

The God, who never looks away.

He saw Hagar in the wilderness.

He saw Joseph in the pit.

He saw Daniel in the furnace.

He saw five boys in a courtroom, no one else wanted to see.

And He sees us.

But… When will we stop looking at our own scars long enough to see the hand reaching through the smoke?

When will we see Him…?

CHAPTER 14

The God who Bleeds

Since I began writing this book, one question has followed me:

Why, even when we claim to love God, do we resist obeying Him fully?

Why is there always a seed of hesitation? A whisper of doubt? A subtle rationalization?

The answer lies in what makes us human: freedom.

When God formed humanity from the dust and breathed life into us, He did not create a program — He created a soul. Alive. Relational. Capable of love.

But what was given as a gift becomes our greatest risk. Freedom to choose obedience becomes the temptation to define truth.

Our egos grow fat on the illusion of control, and we forget that the brilliance of our minds — the very logic we so proudly worship — was itself a spark from the Creator's infinite wisdom. We wield it as if it were the source, forgetting that it is merely a reflection.

Doubt, then, becomes the devil's favorite tool. It is subtle — almost gentle at first — but it always begins the same way: *"Did God really say…?"* (Genesis 3:1). That question, whispered first in Eden, still echoes through human history. It caused Eve to reach, Adam to fall, and generations to walk east of Eden, forever chasing shadows of truth while turning away from the Light.

We were given free will and we used it to doubt the authority of the One who gave it to us. What an absurdity and atrocity.

And yet — even here — God's mercy reigns. For though doubt divides, grace redeems.

When God chose to step into human history through Jesus Christ, He did something the human mind struggles to grasp. The infinite became finite, the eternal entered time, and the Creator became creation.

This act alone — the Incarnation — shatters all philosophical categories. It is the deepest expression of love imaginable, and the first layer of the greatest Paradox human mind has ever encountered.

This brings us to one of the most misunderstood passages in all of Scripture:

"But about that day or hour no one knows, not even the angels in heaven, nor the Son, but only the Father." (Mark 13:32; Matthew 24:36)

Skeptics call this a contradiction. They argue that if Jesus were truly God, He could not be ignorant of anything. But to say this, is to misunderstand both: who Jesus is and what He came to do.

From the opening pages of Genesis, God reveals Himself as both transcendent and immanent — above creation yet intimately within it.

In Genesis 1:26, He says, *"Let Us make man in Our image."* The plural form hints at divine fellowship — Father, Son, and Spirit — working in perfect unity.

In Genesis 3:8, He walks in the garden with Adam and Eve, showing that divinity can move among humanity.

In Exodus 3:14, He declares His eternal name to Moses: *"I AM WHO I AM."* That same divine "I AM" would later be spoken by Jesus in John 8:58: *"Before Abraham was, I AM."*

So, when Jesus says, "Only the Father knows," He is not denying His divinity. He is revealing His humility.

In becoming a man, He did not cease to be God — He chose to lay aside His divine privileges (Philippians 2:6–8). He willingly limited His knowledge and power, lead by parental love. He entered our condition completely — not as an actor playing a role, but as one of us — to experience our hunger, fatigue, sorrow, and yes, even our dependence on the Father.

This was not a weakness. It was obedience in its purest form. Jesus lived in perfect submission to the Father's will, showing us how to live by faith and trust — not by sight or certainty.

In that single statement, "only the Father knows," we see the beauty of divine order within the Trinity:

The Father ordains.
The Son obeys and redeems.
The Spirit reveals and empowers.

Far from a contradiction, this verse reveals the depth of divine relationship and the measure of God's humility. It shows that the Almighty, who spoke galaxies into existence, was willing to live within the same boundaries as His creation — to be hungry, tired, tempted, and tested — so that no human could ever say, "God does not understand me."

He understands — not from afar, but from within.

This is the heart of the Gospel: that God's love is not only infinite — it is intimate. He did not send another prophet to explain Himself. He, Himself came, clothed in flesh, to walk the dusty roads of our confusion and pain, to show us that the way to victory is through surrender.

And when He said He did not know the hour, it was not a confession of ignorance — it was a declaration of humanity. In His humility, He was already pointing us back to the Father, teaching us that the highest wisdom is not to know everything, but to trust the One who does.

There is only ONE time Jesus cries out in anguish – not when his flesh is separated from his back by the lashes, not when the thorns of the mocking crown pierced his forehead, not when the nails cut through his palms and feet, not when he was scorned, spit at, insulted, beaten, abandoned by his people, but at this short amount of time when darkness covered him – this time when the veil was sealed and God withdrew from Earth, leaving His son to be completely Human and letting Him experience the greatest of ALL pain – the complete separation from God! To carry the entire Sin of humanity. Because only this way could our sin have been fully paid.

"My God, my God, why have you forsaken me?" Matthew 27:46, Mark 15:34

Jesus enters the deepest place we fear. Not physical pain, not humiliation, not death itself, but the terror of absent God. The ache we carry when heaven feels silent. God took this terror on Himself through his Son.

This is where obedience ceases to be theory and becomes trust.

Jesus does not obey because He sees the outcome. He obeys because He knows the Father. And in doing so, He sanctifies every human moment where faith must move without certainty. Every time we follow God without understanding. Every time we choose obedience without answers. Every time we stand in a fire that does not recede.

The God who bleeds does not ask us to suffer alone. He asks us to follow Him so that pain no longer has the final word.

Obedience is not submission to power, but participation in love. The Cross shows a God willing to suffer and die for us, rather than live without us.

CHAPTER 15

The Bridge Between Suffering and Glory

The humility of God — the God who limits Himself for love — is the key to understanding pain.

In the light of Christ, pain is not punishment. It is participation. But only when it is surrendered to Him.

To follow Jesus is not merely to believe in His resurrection, but to walk the road that led there. Not to admire the Cross from a safe distance, but to pass beneath its shadow and discover that it does not end in death. *"Unless a grain of wheat falls into the earth and dies," Jesus said, "it remains alone; but if it dies, it bears much fruit."* (John 12:24)

Pain, in the economy of God, is never an end. It is a passage.

The apostle Paul understood this with terrifying clarity when he spoke of his desire not only to know the power of Christ's resurrection, but also the fellowship of His sufferings — to be shaped, even conformed, by a death that leads to life. Resurrection power is not accessed through avoidance. It is entered through surrender.

Suffering, when united with Christ rather than resisted in pride, becomes soil. And in that soil, faith grows roots deeper than comfort ever could.

Sorrow and pain are not God's will. And none of it is beyond His redemption.

Long before Christ took on flesh, Isaiah saw a Messiah who would redeem not through domination, but through grief — despised, rejected, acquainted with torment. One who would be wounded not for His own crimes, but for ours. Crushed not by accident or fate, but by willing obedience.

His suffering did not signal divine failure. It revealed divine love.

By His wounds, healing would enter the world.

Christ embodies the greatest paradox of Pain: what was meant to destroy becomes the instrument of restoration. The Cross was the axis on which history turned.

Jesus did not suffer because the Father lost control. He suffered because love refused to remain distant. He did not numb pain or anesthetize suffering. He absorbed it fully — betrayal, abandonment, humiliation, physical agony, and finally the terror of separation. When darkness covered the land and He cried out that He was forsaken, Jesus named the deepest human fear so that no one would ever suffer it alone again. In that moment, pain ceased to be merely something endured and became something declared: God does not save us from suffering by force; He saves us through it by presence.

This truth becomes personal in Peter.

When Jesus told Peter that he would deny Him three times, it was not a prediction meant to shame or expose him. It was a revelation of how deeply God understands the human condition — and how secure the finished work already was, even before failure entered the story. God was not surprised by Peter. He is never surprised by us.

Jesus did not speak those words hoping they would not come true. He spoke, because they would — and because they needed to. Not because God desired Peter's collapse, but because redemption is not built on human strength. Peter's confidence in his loyalty had to fall so that his confidence in grace could be born. Peter believed he would stand when others fell. Jesus knew better—not because Peter lacked love, but because he was human. God remembers that we are dust. The gospel was never built on Peter's endurance. It was built on Christ's completion.

The denial did not derail the plan. It unveiled it.

Before the failure ever occurred, Jesus had already prayed — not that Peter would never stumble, but that his faith would survive the stagger. Even on the Cross, Jesus did not pray for escape, but for endurance. This is the heart of the Father. After the Resurrection, restoration came without interrogation. Jesus did not rehearse Peter's shame. He did not ask why he failed. He asked one question — three times — not to reopen the wound, but to heal it: Do you love *Me?* Grace does not circle failure. It redeems it.

This pattern did not end with the apostles.

The early martyrs understood something the world still struggles to grasp - when death is no longer feared, power loses its grip. Men and women sang as they were burned, prayed as they were torn apart, and forgave as they were executed — not because they were numb, but because fear had been disarmed. They overcame, Scripture says, not by violence or escape, but by the blood of the Lamb and by the word of their testimony. They did not cling to life as an idol. And because of that, death could no longer rule them.[18]

Their suffering was not spectacle. It was proclamation.

And this is not ancient history. Across the world today, believers are imprisoned, beaten, silenced, and killed — not for crimes, but for confession. And yet the Church grows fastest where it is most opposed. Testimony multiplies where persecution intensifies. Pain becomes seed. Fear loses its final word. Here, suffering no longer asks where God is. It declares that He is worth everything.

Seen in this light, the human story becomes painfully clear:

Every truth given by God, we bent into distortion. Every gift - we sharpened into a weapon.

He gave us identity, and we turned it into pride. Desire, and we twisted it into adultery. Love, and we trained it to hate. Discernment, and we hardened it into judgment. Freedom, and we forged chains for one another. He gave us fear to recognize danger, and we turned it into paralysis. Abundance, and we turned it into greed. Fire to warm and refine, and we turned it into destruction.

He gave us vision to see truth, and we turned it into illusion and vanity. Words to bless and heal, and we used them to curse and divide. Authority to serve, and we converted it into control. Borders for protection, and we turned them into walls of exclusion. Time as a gift, and we wasted it chasing dust. Hands to build and comfort, and we raised them in violence.

He gave us the Cross — the ultimate act of love — and we reduced it to symbol, slogan, or offense, forgetting the blood, the humility, the surrender.

And still — He gives.

Mercy after mercy.

Breath after breath.

Morning after morning.

Not because we deserve it, but because He is faithful even when we

18. Revelation 12:11. "They triumphed over him by the blood of the Lamb and by the word of their testimony; they did not love their lives so much as to shrink from death."

are not.

The apostle Paul wrote in Philippians 3:10,

"That I may know Him and the power of His resurrection, and the fellowship of His sufferings, being made conformable unto His death."

To *know* Christ is not only to share in His resurrection — it is to walk the path that led there: the path of surrender, obedience, and sacrifice. Our sufferings become sacred when we see them as the ground where faith takes root. In the soil of pain, trust grows deepest.

Centuries before Christ came, the prophet Isaiah foresaw this mystery in words that still shake the soul:

"He was despised and rejected by men,
a man of sorrows, and acquainted with grief...
But He was pierced for our transgressions,
He was crushed for our iniquities;
the punishment that brought us peace was on Him,
and by His wounds we are healed." (Isaiah 53:3–5)

Here lies the paradox: *the wounds of Christ became the doorway to our healing; His sorrow became the seed of our joy.* Through pain, we learn the heart of God — not as a distant ruler, but as a suffering Savior.

Every tear shed in surrender, every ache offered in faith, becomes a quiet echo of Calvary — where love triumphed not by power, but by pain.

And so, the story of the Trinity — the Father's will, the Son's obedience, the Spirit's revelation — finds its perfect reflection in us when we choose to surrender.

For in suffering, we are not forsaken.

We are being formed.

That is the paradox of pain: that the very thing meant to break us becomes the thing that brings us home.

One must die to be born again.

A DECLARATION OF ALLEGIANCE

"But if serving the LORD seems undesirable to you, then choose for yourselves this day whom you will serve, whether the gods your ancestors served beyond the Euphrates, or the gods of the Amorites, in whose land you are living. But as for me and my household, we will serve the LORD." — Joshua 24:15 (NIV)

Pain demands allegiance.
Fear demands allegiance.
Pride demands allegiance.
The world offers a thousand idols to numb, distract, or explain away suffering.

But only one path transforms it.

Joshua understood the paradox: God does not promise a painless life — He promises a *purposeful one*. He does not remove death — He redeems it. He does not force our loyalty —
He invites it. And so, Joshua draws a line with his voice:

"Choose today."

Not tomorrow. Not when the storm passes. Not when life feels easier. Today.

Because every day we serve something — fear or faith, sin or salvation, our own will or God's.

Joshua's final words become a spiritual spine for anyone walking through the fire of suffering:
"But as for me and my house,
we will serve the Lord."

It is more than devotion. It is defiance — against the darkness of the

world, the deception of sin,
the illusion of control.

To serve the Lord is to choose life over despair, light - over shadows, eternity - over decay.

It is to say:
"There's a line in the sand, and I'll cross it,
Every whisper of doubt burned away.
From the ashes I'll rise even higher,
In God's light, I will stand and stay."
("I am Made New" – see Appendix II)

And in this choice, death loses its grip.
Suffering loses its final word.
And the soul becomes unbreakable.

CHAPTER 16

GRACE — When Heaven Interrupts

Grace is not a concept. It is a movement. It is heaven leaning toward earth. It is God stepping into the space between what we deserve and what He gives.

Grace is not earned.
It is not negotiated.
It is not scheduled.

It arrives.

Sometimes as comfort.
Sometimes as conviction.
Sometimes as interruption.

***

It was Sunday, October 19, 2025. Church time.

My alarm went off, and I began negotiating with obedience — the quiet way we all do. I told myself I was tired. I told myself I could watch a sermon online. I told myself God would understand.

And then came the nudge.

Not loud. Not dramatic. Just clear.

Go.

I was still in my pajamas. I really did not want to get dressed. But the nudge kept nudging. I had to say yes.

Nothing spectacular happened that morning. No lightning. No vision. No thunder from heaven. But something shifted inside me and made me move.

Grace was not waiting for me inside the building. Grace met me in the decision.

I have come to understand that grace is not only forgiveness after failure. The Father does not stand at a distance, watching us drift. He interrupts.

Not to shame.

But to rescue.

***

Saul was interrupted. He was certain. Convinced. Righteous in his own eyes. And grace met him not with applause, but with a question:

Why are you persecuting Me?

Saul lost his sight, but what fell away was not vision — it was illusion. Grace did not polish Saul. It broke him open. And when the scales fell, he did not become improved.

He became new.

Grace does not always comfort first.

Sometimes it dismantles.

And then - rebuilds.

***

I have learned something else.

Grace does not sanctify every road we walk. It rescues us from inside them. As you already know, there were places I wandered searching for peace — places God does not endorse. Yet even there, He did not abandon me. He entered my confusion, my darkness, and pulled me up when the world dragged me down.

Grace does not approve of every altar.

It reclaims the kneeling heart.

***

And yet, we try to contain grace.

We schedule it into holidays.

We compress it into rituals.

We reduce it to memory.

But grace refuses containment.

It interrupts Tuesday mornings.

It interrupts pride.

It interrupts despair.

It interrupts self-sufficiency.

It interrupts the illusion that we can heal ourselves.

Grace is not seasonal.

It is daily bread.

***

Receiving grace is easier than giving it. To receive grace is to admit we need God. To give grace is to resemble Him.

Receiving grace feels like breathing after drowning.

Giving grace feels like handing breath to the one who hurt you.

One humbles.

The other transforms.

And yet, grace given is where heaven touches earth most visibly.

***

Looking back, I see a pattern. Every time I drifted, grace interrupted. Every time I hardened, grace pressed. Every time I collapsed, grace held.

Not because I was faithful.

But because He is.

Day after day. Blessing after blessing.

Grace is not proof of our goodness.

It is proof of His.

***

In the end, grace asks only one thing: Stop running. Just stop running.

The Shepherd still searches.
The Father still waits.
The Son still bears scars.
The Spirit still whispers.
Come home.

A long time ago, I believed happiness was the absence of pain.

Today, I know:
Happiness is pain transformed.

THE END

Is

THE BEGINNING

APPENDIX I - Questions and Answers

On Questions, Faith, and the Courage to Seek

This appendix was not written to win arguments. It was written because love asks questions.

It was born from a real conversation with someone dear to me — a thoughtful, sincere soul who believes deeply, but differently. She spoke of energy. Of a universal force named differently by cultures — Jesus, Buddha, Krishna, Allah. She rejected punishment, prohibition, dogma. She believed in goodness — but not in a personal, revealed God.

Her words were not hostile. They were honest.

So, I asked questions.

If reality is ultimately impersonal energy, can that energy love? Can it speak? Can it forgive? Can it enter history? Can it suffer? Can it redeem us?

If belief in a personal God requires trust, does belief in an impersonal force require less?

Her final answer was equally sincere: "I do not know."

And that is where this appendix begins.

Christianity does make an exclusive claim. It does not say that every spiritual intuition points to the same reality under different names. It says that God has revealed Himself — not as symbol, not as metaphor, but as a Person who entered history. Talked to us. Bled. Died. Rose.

This section does not assume belief.

It takes doubt seriously.

It does not attempt to answer every objection. That would be impossible and is not needed. Instead, it addresses some of the most common and emotionally charged questions — the ones asked by skeptics, critics, and seekers alike.

You may notice that certain answers return to the same foundational truths. That is not evasion. It is coherence. Truth does not need to reinvent itself for every new challenge. It remains steady, examined from different angles.

God is not threatened by inquiry. Honest seeking will not lead away from Him — but toward Him. So, these pages are not the end of the conversation.

They are its continuation.

About Scripture & Truth

Q1. How do we know the Bible is truly the Word of God — and not simply a human book shaped by power, politics, or tradition?

This question matters because it reaches beneath doctrine and touches authority itself. If Scripture is merely a human product, then it carries no more moral weight than any other ancient text — interesting, perhaps influential, but ultimately negotiable. If it is the Word of God, then it does not submit to power; it stands in judgment over it.

The Bible does not present itself as a book that emerged from a single ruler, council, or political agenda. It is a library of writings composed over roughly fifteen centuries by authors from radically different backgrounds — shepherds, kings, priests, prophets, fishermen, exiles, and prisoners — writing in different languages, cultures, and political systems.

That diversity alone does not prove divine origin. But it does make a single controlling political agenda unlikely.

If Scripture were primarily a tool of power, its content is an unusual choice. It does not protect its heroes. It exposes them.

It records David's adultery and murder.

It chronicles Solomon's corruption.

It recounts Peter's denial.

It preserves Israel's rebellion.

It condemns religious hypocrisy in language sharper than any external critic ever used.

Propaganda shields its leaders.

Scripture indicts them.

The prophets did not gain safety or influence by speaking; they were often persecuted for it. The apostles did not secure political authority; most were executed. Jesus Himself was condemned by both religious and political authorities — not for leading a military revolt, but for undermining the very assumptions that sustain systems of control.

That does not automatically prove inspiration. But it complicates the claim that the Bible was crafted to consolidate power.

Another consideration is coherence.

Across centuries, genres, and authors, Scripture unfolds a continuous narrative: creation, fracture, covenant, failure, promise, redemption — culminating not in a conquering emperor, but in a crucified Messiah. A suffering Savior is not an obvious invention for advancing institutional dominance. In the ancient world, crucifixion was a symbol of humiliation and defeat.

If human ambition were designing the climax, the cross would be a strange centerpiece.

Of course, the Bible was written by human authors. The real question is whether something more than human intention is present within it.

Biblical inspiration does not mean mechanical dictation. It means divine truth conveyed through human language, culture, and personality — much like light passing through stained glass. The glass remains fully itself; yet the source of illumination lies beyond it.

Historical reliability, manuscript preservation, and archaeological corroboration strengthen the Bible's credibility, and these deserve serious study. But perhaps the most difficult aspect to dismiss is the way Scripture confronts the human condition.

It does not flatter.

It does not excuse.

It does not bend easily to cultural preference.

Across centuries and civilizations, it names pride, injustice, lust, greed, idolatry, and self-deception with unsettling consistency. It does not simply describe human behavior; it exposes motives beneath it. Readers across cultures report the same experience: being read while reading.

Power typically flatters its audience. Scripture unsettles it.

Tradition often preserves comfort. Scripture repeatedly calls for repentance and transformation — including from those who claim to represent it.

None of these observations force belief. They do, however, invite serious consideration.

The Bible has survived empires, censorship, political misuse, and institutional corruption. It has been weaponized — and yet it continually resurfaces as a text that critiques the very systems that attempt to control it.

A purely human book can inspire.

What remains open to examination is whether any merely human book could sustain this level of internal coherence, moral confrontation, and historical endurance — while consistently placing both rulers and commoners under the same judgment.

The question is not whether the Bible passed through human hands. It clearly did. The deeper question is whether, through those hands, a voice greater than them continues to speak.

***

Q 2. Has the Bible been altered, edited, or corrupted over time? If so, how can we trust it?

The important question is not whether the Bible has been copied, transmitted, and compiled. It has. Every ancient text has. The real question is whether those processes changed its message in any meaningful way.

The Bible did not survive in a single official copy guarded by one empire or religious authority. It exists in thousands of manuscripts across different regions, languages, and centuries. That multiplicity is not a liability; it is the very mechanism that allows comparison.

If a text were tightly controlled in one location, alteration could go undetected. Because biblical manuscripts were widely dispersed, variations can be identified and examined. Textual differences do exist — but their nature matters.

The overwhelming majority of variants involve spelling, word order, or minor scribal clarifications. Ancient Greek, for example, allows flexible word order without changing meaning. Where larger variations appear, they are not hidden. They are documented, footnoted, and openly discussed in modern critical editions of Scripture. No central doctrine of Christianity rests on a disputed passage.

The accusation of corruption also raises a historical question: Who altered it — and to what end?

In the earliest centuries, Christians had no centralized political power, no unified institutional structure, and no ability to impose a standardized text across the Roman Empire. Many of them were persecuted minorities. The writings they preserved repeatedly placed them at odds with both religious authorities and imperial systems. They preserved accounts of their leaders' failures, warnings against false authority, and teachings that invited suffering rather than dominance.

It is difficult to identify a clear motive or mechanism for large-scale theological alteration in that context.

The formation of the biblical canon likewise did not occur by sudden political decree. Over time, Christian communities recognized certain writings as apostolic, consistent with received teaching, and widely used in worship. Church councils did not invent Scripture; they affirmed what had already been functioning as Scripture among diverse communities.

The discovery of the Dead Sea Scrolls provides additional historical perspective. Manuscripts of the Hebrew Scriptures dating nearly a thousand years earlier than previously known copies demonstrate remarkable continuity. Variations exist — as expected in hand-copied texts — but no evidence of wholesale theological rewriting.

Trust, therefore, does not rest on the unrealistic assumption that transmission occurred without any human imperfection. It rests on the cumulative evidence that, despite normal scribal variation, the central narrative and theological claims of Scripture have remained stable.

The Bible has been handled.

It has been copied, studied, debated, translated.

But there is no compelling historical evidence that its core message was systematically altered to serve hidden agendas.

What remains today is substantially the same message that early Jewish and Christian communities read, preserved, and often suffered to protect.

***

Q3. What about forcing people to become Christians?

This question often arises next, and it is important to address it honestly: Forced conversion is incompatible with Christianity as taught by Christ.

Jesus did not compel belief. He invited people. He taught. He warned. When some rejected Him, He did not coerce them. When His disciples suggested calling down judgment on those who refused Him, He rebuked them. When followers walked away, He did not chase them with force.

Faith, by definition, cannot be manufactured through violence. Coercion can produce conformity. But never conviction.

Historically, forced conversions occurred not in the vulnerable, persecuted early church, but after Christianity became intertwined with political power. When empire and church became entangled, religion was sometimes used as an instrument of control. Those actions reflect the misuse of Christian identity — not the teachings of Christ Himself.

The New Testament repeatedly warns against false shepherds, corrupt leaders, and those who invoke God while betraying His character. The existence of abuse does not invalidate the standard by which that abuse is judged.

When Christians have forced belief, they have acted contrary to the very Scriptures they claim to defend.

The abuse of a name does not define the truth of that name.

Christianity stands or falls on the life and teachings of Jesus — not on the historical failures of those who claimed to represent Him.

***

Q4. What about wars fought in the name of Christ?

Clarity is essential here: Wars have indeed been fought under the banner of Christ. But they were not fought because of His teachings; they were fought while borrowing His name.

Jesus taught love of enemies, rejection of revenge, and willingness to suffer rather than dominate. He refused political kingship. He rebuked violence in His defense. He submitted to execution rather than inflict it.

No empire is built on that ethic.

When wars are fought "in the name of Christ," the name functions as a banner, not a source. Christ becomes a symbol to rally power, not a Lord to obey. The tension is not subtle; it is foundational.

It is also important to recognize that Scripture itself anticipates this misuse. The prophets repeatedly condemn those who invoke God's authority while practicing injustice. Their sharpest rebukes are directed not at outsiders, but at those who claim covenant privilege while violating covenant law.

If Christianity were designed to justify holy war, its center would not be a crucified Messiah who forbade violence in His defense.

The historical failures of Christians must be acknowledged. But those failures stand in contradiction to Christ's explicit teaching, not as its fulfillment.

***

Q5. What about the books that were "deleted" from the Bible?

This claim often assumes that a complete Bible once existed and that certain books were later removed to suppress inconvenient ideas. There is no historical evidence of such a process.

What existed in the early centuries was not a fixed table of contents, but a wide range of writings circulating among different communities. The question Christians faced was not "Which books should we delete?" but "Which writings faithfully preserve apostolic teaching?"

The books eventually recognized as Scripture shared several characteristics:

They traced to apostolic authority or close eyewitness testimony.

They were consistent with the core message already received.

They were widely used across diverse communities, not confined to a single sect.

Other writings were not hidden secrets. Many still exist and are studied today. They were known in antiquity, read in some circles, and debated. But they were ultimately regarded as later compositions, speculative expansions, or theological reinterpretations.

Many of these excluded texts reflect attempts to reshape Jesus in ways more aligned with later philosophical or mystical movements. Some elevate secret knowledge. Others soften the outrage of the cross or distance Jesus from real human suffering.

The canonical texts, by contrast, preserve a Messiah who is crucified, not merely enlightened; incarnate, not merely symbolic; publicly executed, not privately decoded.

If church authorities had been curating Scripture for comfort or control, they might have omitted passages that condemn religious hypocrisy, expose leadership failure, and insist that God sides with the weak rather than the powerful. Those elements remain.

The formation of the canon was not an act of erasure. It was a process of recognition — acknowledging the writings that had already shaped and governed the faith of widespread communities.

***

Q6. If people keep corrupting faith, why does God allow His name to be misused at all?

This question moves from history into theology.

Scripture presents a God who values genuine love over forced allegiance. Genuine love requires freedom — including the freedom to misuse what is holy.

From the beginning, God commands faithfulness but does not manufacture it. He allows His name to be spoken sincerely and insincerely. He allows hypocrisy to surface rather than suppressing it by force.

If God prevented the misuse of His name through immediate intervention, He would also eliminate the possibility of authentic trust. What would remain is outward compliance, not inward transformation.

This is not indifference. It is restraint.

Throughout Scripture, God permits His covenant people to misrepresent Him — sometimes gravely. The prophets confront this directly. The misuse of God's name is treated as serious precisely because it distorts truth at its source.

Why, then, is judgment not always immediate?

Because immediate correction would collapse history into coercion. Instead, God allows time — time for exposure, repentance, and distinction between genuine faith and counterfeit allegiance.

A lie may invoke God's name.

It cannot sustain God's character.

The cross reveals this most clearly. The crucifixion itself is the ultimate instance of God's name being used to justify injustice. Religious authorities invoked divine law to condemn the Son of God. God did not prevent it — not because He approved, but because He intended to expose the depth of human corruption and reveal a deeper redemption.

The cross shows that even the worst misuse of faith cannot overturn God's purposes. False religion is allowed to speak fully — and in doing so, it reveals itself.

If God were primarily concerned with protecting reputation, the crucifixion would have been prevented. Instead, He chose to vindicate truth through resurrection rather than through immediate force.

Scripture does not promise a world in which God's name is never abused. It promises that every misuse will ultimately be exposed and judged. Until then, faith is not measured by how loudly God's name is invoked, but by how faithfully His character is reflected.

That distinction — between name and nature — is where accountability begins.

***

Q7. Why does the Bible sometimes appear contradictory or morally troubling when read at face value?

Because the Bible is not a single-voice moral handbook suspended in abstraction. It is a revelatory record unfolding across history, speaking into fractured cultures, moral collapse, and human limitation — often without sanitizing the mess.

At face value, Scripture can appear contradictory because it speaks progressively, contextually, and honestly about human failure rather than presenting idealized behavior. Several clarifications help:

The Bible describes evil without endorsing it

One of the most common mistakes is assuming that what the Bible records, it approves.

Example: Polygamy

Scripture records polygamy among patriarchs and kings, but it never presents it as God's design. Every polygamous household is marked by jealousy, rivalry, injustice, or grief. The narrative rarely pauses to moralize in modern language — it allows consequences to reveal the truth.

A troubling text may be troubling precisely because it is honest.

God works within broken systems before dismantling them

Scripture often regulates evil before it eradicates it. Immediate abolition, in certain ancient contexts, could collapse societies without transforming hearts.

Example: Slavery

Biblical laws restrict brutality, protect basic dignity, and limit exploitation in cultures where slavery was universal. Later revelation condemns man-stealing explicitly and frames freedom as part of God's redemptive arc. This is not contradiction but moral movement.

God meets humanity where it is — not where it imagines itself to be.

Moral clarity unfolds across revelation

What appears contradictory is often developmental.

Example: Violence

Early Israel's warfare is regulated. Prophets increasingly condemn injustice and bloodshed. Christ rejects violence as a means of advancing God's kingdom.

The trajectory moves from containment to confrontation to transformation.

Truth deepens in expression without changing in essence.

Scripture preserves tension deliberately

The Bible does not rush to resolve every moral discomfort.

Example: Job

Job suffers unjustly. God never provides a direct explanation. The problem is not solved, it is exposed. Scripture sometimes withholds answers to prevent us from worshiping explanation rather than God.

Many "contradictions" reflect moral complexity

Tensions often sit between justice and mercy; judgment and patience; holiness and compassion. For example:

God judges injustice.

God forgives the guilty.

Both are true — and neither cancels the other.

A God who never judges would not be good.

A God who never forgives would not be merciful.

Scripture refuses to collapse complexity into slogans.

The most troubling texts reveal the seriousness of evil

Passages such as the Flood, Sodom, or Jerusalem's destruction disturb us because they portray judgment as the culmination of persistent corruption, not arbitrary cruelty. They are presented as severe, reluctant, and preceded by warning.

The Bible does not treat evil as harmless.

It shows its trajectory.

The cross reframes everything

If Scripture were merely a moral rulebook, its hardest passages would condemn it. But instead, Scripture culminates not in domination, but in God absorbing judgment Himself.

The cross does not erase difficult texts. It reveals that God takes evil seriously enough to confront it — and humanity seriously enough to redeem it.

In summary

The Bible often appears contradictory or morally troubling when: we expect it to affirm modern sensibilities; when we read it as static law instead of unfolding revelation; when we mistake description for endorsement, or demand comfort where Scripture insists on truth.

The Bible is not written to protect our moral confidence. It is written to expose, confront, and ultimately heal.

And that is precisely why it resists reading like propaganda.

***

Q8. Why does Christianity look like propaganda to many unbelievers?

When unbelievers call Christianity propaganda, they are often reacting to how it has been presented, not necessarily to what Scripture contains.

Christianity has indeed been used as propaganda. Empires have borrowed its language. Institutions have wrapped themselves in its authority. Leaders have invoked God to silence opposition. That misuse should be rejected.

The deeper question is whether the Bible itself functions as propaganda. And the answer is that when examined closely, it fails the basic tests of effective propaganda.

What does propaganda do and what Scripture does not:

Propaganda protects its founders and heroes

Scripture does the opposite.
Abraham lies.
Moses disobeys.
David commits adultery and orchestrates murder.
Peter denies Jesus publicly.
The disciples misunderstand and flee.
A propaganda text would edit this out.

Scripture preserves it.

Propaganda flatters the in-group

The Bible repeatedly indicts its own people.

Israel is called stubborn and unjust.

Religious leaders receive the harshest rebukes.

Jesus reserves His strongest words for the devout, not outsiders.

Propaganda praises insiders.

Scripture warns them.

Propaganda justifies power

The New Testament centers on a Messiah who rejects political kingship, rebukes violence, and accepts execution rather than seize authority.

A crucified Savior does not serve imperial messaging.

It undermines it.

Propaganda suppresses doubt

Scripture canonizes doubt and protest.

Job questions God.

The Psalms lament divine silence.

Ecclesiastes wrestles with meaninglessness.

Thomas doubts resurrection.

These voices are not erased. They are included.

Propaganda simplifies morality

Scripture refuses reduction. It holds together justice and mercy, judgment and patience, divine sovereignty and human responsibility.

This complexity frustrates readers — precisely because it resists slogan.

Why then, the accusation persists?

Because Christianity has often been presented as a tool of control. That historical misuse is real. But the existence of misuse does not define the nature of the text itself.

The Bible predicts religious hypocrisy. It condemns those who invoke God falsely. It warns that misusing God's name invites severe judgment.

A book designed to control populations would not center on a publicly humiliated Messiah executed by both religious and political authorities.

***

Q9. If God wanted to be known, why didn't He make His revelation simpler and universally obvious?

Because being known is not the same as being acknowledged — and neither is the same as relationship. If God's existence were psychologically unavoidable — as obvious as gravity — faith would cease to be meaningful. Compliance would replace trust.

Obviousness does not create love

Coercion produces conformity, not devotion. Surveillance produces behavior, not virtue. God's restraint protects freedom. Even when God acts visibly through miracles or judgment, people still resist. Obviousness does not heal the will.

God makes Himself knowable, not unavoidable

Scripture presents creation, conscience, moral law, history, and Christ as witness — not compulsion. They invite. They confront. They do not override.

The Bible speaks of hardened hearts and willful blindness. The issue is rarely lack of information. It is resistance to implication.

Simplicity would distort reality

We assume ultimate truth should be simple. Yet love, justice, and human motivation are not simple.

Why should God be?

A reduced, simplified deity would become manageable — more principle than Person. Scripture resists that reduction.

God is not a formula. He is a moral reality.

Universal obviousness would empower control

If God were undeniable in a measurable, scientific sense, the powerful would mediate access. Institutions would claim exclusive authority to interpret the divine.

History suggests where that leads.

Instead, Scripture repeatedly shows God revealing Himself to the humble, the outsider, the willing — not the dominant.

The cross explains the method

The cross reveals God without overwhelming the will. It does not force acknowledgment.

It asks a question: What kind of God would suffer like this?

That question invites conscience rather than compels submission.

The uncomfortable conclusion

God did not make Himself universally obvious because His goal is not to eliminate disbelief. It is to restore people.

Truth that overwhelms the will produces submission. Truth that invites the will makes relationship possible.

Propaganda shouts to silence resistance. God speaks clearly enough to be found — and quietly enough to be refused.

That restraint reveals something profound about what He values most.

Pause. Reflect. Stand honestly before God.

• When Scripture unsettles something that I deeply hold, do I dismiss it — or do I remain with it until it has spoken fully?

• When I resist the Bible, is my resistance intellectual — or toward the authority it claims over my life?

• Where do I actually seek truth when it matters most?

• Do I examine God's Word carefully and humbly — or do I judge it from a distance?

• When I read Scripture, am I merely studying history — or do I allow myself to be searched and confronted?

• What is faith to me — agreement, comfort, identity, surrender, obedience?

• What do I need to shift in my priorities, attachments, or allegiances?

About Jesus & Salvation

Q10. Why Jesus? Why not another prophet, teacher, or spiritual path?

Christianity does not begin with a philosophy, a mythic archetype, or a timeless spiritual principle. It begins with a claim: that Jesus of Nazareth lived, taught, was executed, and rose from the dead — in a specific place, under a specific government, at a specific moment in history.

This matters because Christianity anchors itself in history, not abstraction. It is not built around a teaching that can be detached from its founder. It is built around a claim about reality — and that claim either stands or collapses with one person: Jesus Christ.

From a distance, many religions appear similar: moral guidance, spiritual discipline, transcendence, peace. At that level, Jesus can seem interchangeable — one teacher among many.

But Christianity is not offering a method.

It is making a claim about truth.

That distinction changes everything.

Jesus' existence is one of the most widely affirmed facts of ancient history

Among professional historians — including secular, Jewish, and non-Christian scholars — the existence of Jesus is not seriously disputed. The debate concerns His identity and the interpretation of His life, not whether He lived.

Jesus is referenced in multiple early sources; written within living memory of the events they describe. These include both sympathetic and unsympathetic voices.

Across those sources, several core facts are broadly recognized: Jesus was a Jewish teacher. He gained a following. He was associated with unusual deeds. He was executed under Roman authority. His followers claimed He rose from the dead and continued asserting that claim at significant personal cost.

These are historical observations, not theological declarations.

Non-Christian sources acknowledge Jesus

Writers who were neither Christian nor supportive of Christianity mention Jesus and His execution.[19] They do not affirm His divinity. They do not defend His followers. But they confirm His existence and crucifixion.

This is significant.

Christianity did not invent Jesus in isolation. It emerged in the presence of hostile witnesses who could have denied His existence — but did not.

The disagreement has never been about whether Jesus lived. It has always been about who He was.

Islam affirms Jesus as a real historical figure

Islam, emerging centuries later, explicitly affirms Jesus (Isa) as a historical person — a prophet born of the Virgin Mary, performing miracles, and honored by God. Islam rejects the crucifixion and resurrection as Christians understand them. But it does not deny that Jesus lived.

This matters because Islam positions itself within the same historical stream as Judaism and Christianity. If Jesus were purely fictional, denial would have been simple. Instead, Islam reinterprets Him.

The issue again is not existence.

It is identity.

Other traditions reinterpret rather than dismiss Him

In many Hindu and Buddhist contexts, Jesus is acknowledged as a moral teacher or enlightened figure. He is often respected, sometimes incorporated into broader spiritual frameworks.[20]

He is never dismissed as imaginary.

He is reframed.

---

19. Roman historians like Tacitus, Jewish scholars like Josephus, and critics like Lucian of Samosata all acknowledge the same fact: Jesus of Nazareth lived, and He was crucified under Pontius Pilate.

20. **Mahatma Gandhi** (1869–1948), the Indian political leader and Hindu thinker, referred to Jesus as "one of the greatest teachers humanity has ever known."

Swami Vivekananda (1863–1902), founder of the Ramakrishna Mission and one of the most influential Hindu philosophers to introduce Eastern spirituality to the West, described Jesus as a spiritually realized yogi and divine soul.

Paramahansa Yogananda (1893–1952), author of Autobiography of a Yogi and founder of the Self-Realization Fellowship, taught that Jesus was a realized master who understood and embodied divine consciousness.

Sri Ramakrishna (1836–1886), the Bengali mystic whose teachings inspired the Ramakrishna movement, regarded Jesus as one of many manifestations of the Divine.

Tenzin Gyatso (b. 1935), the 14th Dalai Lama and the most influential contemporary Buddhist spiritual leader, has described Jesus as either a bodhisattva or a highly enlightened being. In Buddhist thought, a bodhisattva is one who postpones final enlightenment in order to help others attain liberation.

Thich Nhat Hanh (1926–2022), the Vietnamese Zen Buddhist monk and influential spiritual teacher, wrote that "Jesus and Buddha are brothers," emphasizing parallels between their teachings on compassion and peace.

When a figure is fictional, traditions deny existence.

When a figure is disruptive but historically anchored, traditions re-interpret.

Christianity invites historical examination

Christianity openly ties its truth claims to historical events — named rulers, named places, public execution, public proclamation of resurrection.

Jesus is not just one option among many. Christianity exists because of Him. Other spiritual paths often present wisdom that can, at least in theory, be detached from its founder and still remain intact as a system of practice or philosophy.

Christianity cannot.

Remove Jesus, and you do not have a modified Christianity. You have no Christianity at all.

That is not insulation from scrutiny.

It is exposure to it.

Christianity hands you the fulcrum and says: Test it! Examine this man.

If He did not live, the claim collapses.

If He did not rise, the claim collapses.

If He is not who He said He was, the claim collapses.

The question is not whether Jesus was wise.

It is whether He is Lord.

And that is not a philosophical preference.

It is a historical and existential decision of truth.

***

Q11. What about people born into other religions — are they automatically condemned?

No. And Scripture is far more careful here than many of its loudest defenders — or critics — have been. Christianity does not teach that geography, culture, or inherited religion automatically damn a person. That idea belongs to fear-driven religion, not to the biblical witness.

The Bible rejects "guilt by birth"

Scripture does not operate on tribal fatalism. People are not condemned for circumstances they did not choose.

The consistent biblical pattern is this: Accountability corresponds to light received. Responsibility increases with knowledge. Judgment is based on response, not mere exposure.

A God who condemned people for accidents of birth would be unjust. And Scripture repeatedly insists that God is not unjust.

God judges response, not religious label

The Bible distinguishes between: rejecting truth knowingly and ever encountering it clearly. Those are not treated as morally identical.

Scripture portrays God responding to people outside covenant structures — outside Israel, outside formal revelation — according to conscience, humility, and their response to the good they know.

This dismantles the caricature of automatic condemnation.

Jesus disrupts simplistic "insider vs. outsider" salvation

Jesus repeatedly unsettles religious certainty.

He praises faith in outsiders.

He rebukes hypocrisy in insiders.

He insists that proximity to religion is not the same as alignment with God.

If salvation were about affiliation alone, Jesus' harshest warnings would not be directed at the religious — yet they are.

That is not incidental. It is central.

The tension Scripture refuses to collapse

Christianity does not say: all paths are equally true, belief is irrelevant, or truth is subjective. But neither does it say that ignorance automatically condemns; that God delights in exclusion; or that exposure alone determines destiny.

Instead, Scripture holds three truths together:

God desires all to be saved.

God judges justly.

God knows the heart.

It does not resolve this into a neat formula — because formulas are tools of human control. Judgment is entrusted to a personal, morally consistent God.

Condemnation is tied to rejection of light

The strongest language of judgment in Scripture is directed toward hypocrisy, willful blindness, misuse of truth, and religious arrogance. Not toward sincere seekers born into other traditions.

In fact, Scripture warns that those with the greatest knowledge bear the greatest responsibility.

That should sober anyone tempted to moral superiority.

Why proclaim Jesus as essential, then?

Because Christianity does not claim: "Everyone who hasn't heard the name of Jesus is automatically condemned."

It claims: Jesus is the fullest revelation of who God is.

The New Testament insists that reconciliation ultimately flows through Christ — because God has chosen to reveal Himself there. How this applies to those who never encountered Him clearly is entrusted to divine justice, not human speculation.

And Scripture is explicit: God's judgment is not mechanical. *It is personal.*

What about those who seek but cannot believe?

The Bible does not treat sincere seeking as rebellion. Nor does it equate faith with instant certainty. It distinguishes between inability to believe and refusal to seek.

Its sharpest warnings are aimed not at doubters, but at those who use certainty — or skepticism — to avoid truth.

Seeking in Scripture is relational, not performative. It is orientation, not instant conclusion. Knocking. Waiting. Remaining open.

God is not limited by cognitive barriers, trauma, or distorted exposure to religion. He judges with full knowledge of the heart.

But Scripture also warns us: it is possible to say "I want truth" while protecting what one is unwilling to surrender.

We may deceive ourselves.

We cannot deceive God.

The biblical pattern remains consistent: Sincere seeking does not end in silence. God does not promise immediate clarity. He promises faithful encounter. Not by force. Not on demand. But persistently.

***

Q12. Isn't Christianity just one religion among many — and a relatively young one?

This question assumes that all religions are fundamentally offering variations of the same thing — different cultural expressions of one ultimate reality. If that were true, Christianity would indeed be one option among many. But Christianity's claim is categorically different. It does not claim to be the oldest tradition, the most refined philosophy, or the most disciplined spiritual path.

It claims that something happened in history.

Islam — Submission to God vs. God's self-giving

Islam centers on submission to the will of a sovereign, transcendent God. Revelation is instruction: law, guidance, command. God sends guidance. Humanity obeys.

Christianity makes a different claim: God does not remain solely transcendent. He enters history. He takes on flesh. He absorbs the consequence of human failure.

Islam emphasizes divine sovereignty and human submission. Christianity emphasizes divine self-giving love, culminating in the cross.

Obedience in Christianity is real — but it is response to grace, not the condition for earning mercy.

This is not a minor variation. It is a different direction of movement.

<u>Buddhism — Escape from suffering vs. redemption of suffering</u>

Buddhism diagnoses suffering as central to human experience and seeks liberation through detachment and enlightenment. Suffering is transcended. Desire is relinquished. The self is ultimately dissolved.

Christianity does not bypass suffering. It claims God enters it. Jesus does not teach detachment from pain. He inhabits it.

The cross is not an escape from suffering. It is God within suffering.

The self is not erased. It is redeemed.

<u>Hinduism — Cycles of reality vs. historical interruption</u>

Hindu thought presents reality as cyclical: creation, destruction, rebirth. The central problem is ignorance. Liberation is a release from illusion and reunion with ultimate reality.

Christianity rejects cyclical time. It claims history moves toward resolution — and that God acts decisively within history, not merely through cosmic process.

Jesus is not presented as one manifestation among many. He is presented as a singular historical event.

That claim is not philosophical aggression.

It is historical specificity.

The decisive difference

Many religious systems offer a path to follow. A discipline to practice. A method to ascend.

Christianity begins with a declaration: Something has already been done.

It does not begin with human ascent toward God.
It begins with divine descent into human brokenness.

Not as a metaphor.

Not as an distant force.

But as a person who claims to be God — and stakes that claim on resurrection.

That claim is either false.

Or it changes the world.

***

Q13. What proves that Jesus is God?

Christianity does not rest this claim on wishful thinking or late mythmaking. It rests on four interlocking realities:

What Jesus claimed

How He acted

How His contemporaries understood Him

What happened after His death

No single strand proves divinity on its own. Together, they demand a verdict.

Jesus claimed authority that belongs to God alone

Jesus did not speak merely as a prophet delivering God's words. Prophets say, "Thus says the Lord." Jesus says, *"I say to you."*

He forgave sins committed against others, reinterpreted sacred law around Himself, claimed authority over judgment and eternal destiny, identified Himself with *"I AM"* — the divine name revealed in Exodus.

In a first-century Jewish context fiercely protective of monotheism, these were not vague spiritual claims. They were understood as divine claims — which is precisely why they provoked charges of blasphemy.

Jesus acted as God acts in Scripture

Jesus does not merely speak about God — He acts with divine prerogative:

He commands nature.

He heals without invoking another authority.

He restores rather than merely instructs.

He declares final judgment.

And critically, He accepts worship.

Throughout Scripture, angels and apostles immediately reject worship directed toward them. Jesus does not.

Examples:

Thomas: "My Lord and my God." (John 20:28) — Jesus affirms his belief.

The women at the tomb (Matthew 28:9) — He does not rebuke them.

The man born blind (John 9:38) — Worship is accepted.

The disciples in the boat (Matthew 14:33) — No correction given.

The Magi (Matthew 2:11) — Worship offered without protest.

For a first-century Jew, accepting worship was either blasphemy — or truth.

His enemies understood the claim

Jesus was not executed for being a moral teacher. He was executed because His claims were understood as making Himself equal with God.

If Jesus had been misunderstood, He had opportunities to clarify. Instead, He intensified the claim.

The crucifixion was not confusion. It was response.

The resurrection is the hinge

Christianity openly states: If Jesus did not rise from the dead, the faith collapses.

The resurrection is not presented as metaphor or private vision, but as a public event proclaimed immediately in the city of His execution.

The early Christian message was not: "His spirit lives on." It was: "God raised Him from the dead."

And it was proclaimed under threat, imprisonment, and execution.

Historical reasons the resurrection demands explanation

The proclamation is extremely early

The New Testament preserves creedal formulas that scholars — including non-Christian historians — date within a few years of the crucifixion (often AD 30–35). This means resurrection belief was circulating while eyewitnesses were still alive.

Legends require time.

The resurrection claim had none.

The empty tomb

All four Gospels report women as the first witnesses — a detail unlikely to be invented in that culture. If fabricated, male witnesses would have been substituted.

Opponents did not deny the empty tomb. They proposed alternative explanations (e.g., theft). That concedes the tomb was, indeed, empty.

Multiple appearances

Resurrection appearances are reported to individuals, to groups, indoors and outdoors, over time, including by skeptics. Hallucinations are private, subjective, and non-transferable. They do not account for this pattern.

The transformation of the disciples

Before the crucifixion Jesus' followers exhibit fear, denial, flight. After the resurrection - public proclamation, imprisonment, martyrdom.

People may die for beliefs they think are true.

They do not willingly die for what they know is false.

Something happened.

Radical shifts in Jewish belief

First-century Jews did not expect a crucified Messiah, a single resurrection before the end of time, or worship directed toward a human. And yet, these changes occur rapidly.

The resurrection is the most coherent explanation.

The cross redefines God

If Jesus were inventing divinity, the cross is the worst possible strategy. No one fabricating divine authority invents a God who:

Refuses violence;
Accepts humiliation;
Absorbs injustice;
Forgives executioners.
The cross does not look like mythic power.
It looks like revelation.

The hard conclusion

Christianity does not prove Jesus is God through argument alone. It presents a person, a claim, and an event — and asks whether the best explanation of the evidence is that God acted in history.

If Jesus is not God, Christianity should be rejected.

If He is, then the claim is not one religion among many.

It is revelation.

***

Q14. Why is faith in Jesus necessary at all — why not just live a good, moral life?

Christianity does not argue that humanity lacks morals. It argues that humanity is morally fractured. The problem is not ignorance of good. It is inability to live it consistently.

Christianity affirms morality — but questions its sufficiency

The Bible commands justice, mercy, humility, and love. But it observes something universal: Even our best efforts fall short of our own standards.

The issue is not lack of effort.

It is that moral effort cannot undo what has already been done.

Goodness does not erase guilt

If someone commits harm, future goodness does not erase past wrongdoing. Justice does not operate as a balance sheet.

If God is just, goodness cannot simply cancel guilt.

Faith in Jesus addresses this — not by dismissing justice, but by satisfying it through reconciliation.

Jesus intensifies morality

Jesus moves morality from action to intention:

Anger becomes moral failure

Lust becomes moral failure

Pride becomes moral failure

If salvation were earned by morality, Jesus' teaching would make it unattainable.

That is the point.

The core problem is relational, not behavioral

Christianity claims the deepest problem is alienation from God.

You can obey rules and remain distant.

You can perform morally and remain estranged.

Faith is not moral achievement.

It is reconciliation.

"Just be good" assumes neutrality

Christianity denies moral neutrality.

According to Scripture, the human fracture began with deliberate distrust of God — not imposed innocence but chosen autonomy. That rupture reshaped human nature.

We are not neutral beings occasionally failing.

We are compromised beings attempting goodness from within distortion.

"Just be good" assumes the very condition Christianity disputes.

Faith is the source of transformation

Christianity does not say: Believe instead of living well. It says: Believe so that living well becomes possible from within. Good works are consequence, not currency.

Morality without grace produces either pride or despair.

Grace produces humility — and then obedience.

The cross makes morality alone impossible

If moral effort were enough, the cross would be unnecessary. Christianity's most provocative claim is also its most coherent: Human goodness could not repair what was broken. So God acted.

Faith in Jesus is not a substitute for morality.

It is the only foundation that makes lasting morality possible.

The quiet conclusion

In Christianity "Are you good enough?" becomes "Are you willing to be made whole?"

Faith is necessary not because God rejects moral people, but because morality cannot reconcile us to Him.

That is not insult.

It is diagnosis.

Pause. Reflect. Stand honestly before God.

- Who is Jesus for me - have I reduced Him to a teacher I can admire rather than a Lord I must obey?

- Do I approach Christ as an idea to evaluate — or as a reality to whom I must respond?

- When confronted with the cross, do I seek explanation — or do I recognize cost?

- Is salvation something I assume, something I debate, or something I have surrendered into?

- Do I believe people need reconciliation with God, and what in me still resists being reconciled?

- Am I drawn to Jesus for comfort — or for transformation?

- Is Christ at the center of my story?

About God's Character & Morality

Q15. Why does the Bible describe God allowing or regulating slavery? Does God condone it?

No. Scripture does not present slavery as God's moral design. It presents God speaking into a world where slavery already existed—then placing limits on it, restraining cruelty, and planting principles that eventually make slavery morally indefensible.

The distinction matters: regulation is not approval. It is containment of damage inside a fallen world.

Slavery is not introduced by God in the biblical storyline

Bondage appears as a human institution long before Israel receives God's law—tied to war, debt, poverty, and empire. God's commands address what exists; they do not create the institution.

"Slavery" in the ancient world was not one thing

Modern readers often import the categories of race-based, lifelong chattel slavery into every biblical passage. Ancient servitude could include debt labor, temporary indenture, household service with legal protection, and—tragically—war captivity. None of this makes it righteous; it explains why the legal constraints mattered.

Biblical laws restrict power rather than sanctify it

Where Scripture gives statutes about servitude, the movement is consistently toward limiting exploitation:

Kidnapping humans for sale is condemned.

Abuse is punished.

Rest and dignity are mandated.

Release is built into Israel's covenant life.

Masters are made accountable before God.

A law that restrains cruelty is not a moral endorsement of the cruelty it restrains.

Scripture embeds principles slavery cannot survive

From the start, the Bible insists humans bear God's image; that God hears the oppressed; that exploitation is a serious evil; that deliverance is central to His identity (Exodus). By the New Testament, the moral logic intensifies: *the same Lord stands over master and servant,* and man-stealing is treated as wicked. A system built on ownership collapses when moral equality becomes non-negotiable.

Why doesn't God abolish it instantly?

In the ancient economy, immediate abolition would often have produced catastrophes for the already vulnerable—hunger, homelessness, mass instability. Scripture repeatedly shows God restraining evil first, then dismantling it through moral illumination over time. That is not a compromise with evil; it is redemptive patience working within history.

The cross clarifies God's posture toward domination

Christianity is centered on a God who takes the form of a servant, suffers under oppression, and refuses to preserve Himself through violence. The crucified Christ does not defend hierarchy; He exposes and judges it from within.

Conclusion

The Bible does not call slavery good. It calls humanity broken — and shows God meeting that brokenness with restraint, moral pressure, and a long arc toward liberation. The scandal is not that Scripture mentions slavery; it is that it refuses to let ownership, coercion, and exploitation claim final authority.

***

Q16. Why did God require sacrifices—and did He ever require human sacrifice, such as a firstborn son?

Stated plainly: God never required human sacrifice. The sacrificial system was not divine bloodlust. It was a temporary, morally charged framework that confronted sin, guarded the vulnerable, and contradicted pagan religion from the inside out.

Sacrifice wasn't invented by God as a new religious technology

Sacrifice was everywhere in the ancient world—used to manipulate deities, bargain for outcomes, or avert fear. Scripture does something unexpected: it reverses the direction. Sacrifice becomes less about humans controlling God and more about God schooling humans—teaching that wrongdoing is not cosmetic, and reconciliation is not cheap.

Sacrifice makes moral reality visible

Sin is not presented as a mistake in a spreadsheet—it is relational damage with real cost. Sacrifice dramatizes that cost. But Scripture refuses the most horrific pagan conclusion: the vulnerable must pay. In the biblical pattern, the vulnerable are protected, not offered.

"He punishes the children… "—does Scripture teach inherited guilt? (Numbers 14:18)

This is often misunderstood as God morally blaming children for what they didn't do. The Bible's own logic points elsewhere.

Guilt is personal. Moral responsibility belongs to the actor.

Consequences can be inherited. The fallout of a parent's rebellion—poverty, violence, hardened patterns, fear — spills into descendants.

Numbers 14 describes the reach of generational damage when sin is unrepeated, not the transfer of moral blame to innocents. Even the phrasing signals restraint: judgment reaches "third and fourth," while mercy extends vastly farther. And the moment a generation turns, the pattern breaks. The warning is aimed at adults: *your choices shape your children's world.*

The cross resolves the tension decisively: guilt is not pushed onto the weak; it is borne by God Himself.

Animal sacrifice is substitution, not cruelty-as-worship

Scripture is explicit that God does not need offerings to survive or be satisfied. The point is moral and symbolic: life is sacred; sin leads to death; *mercy involves substitution; forgiveness has weight.* This system prepares the mind for the ultimate claim of Christianity: *God Himself will bear what justice requires.*

God repeatedly condemns human sacrifice

Child sacrifice was common among neighboring cultures and often framed as the "highest devotion." Scripture calls it detestable and forbids it. God goes out of His way to draw a line: *animals may be offered; humans may not.*

Abraham and Isaac: the story is designed to break the pagan expectation

This episode is meant to disturb — because it confronts the ancient assumption that gods demand firstborn sons. God stops Abraham. That interruption is the sermon.

The message is not "true faith kills your child."

The message is: *I am not like the gods you have imagined.*

A substitute is provided; the child lives; the logic of child sacrifice is shattered.

"Consecrate the firstborn" (Exodus 13:1–2) — does that imply offering sons?

Read the next instruction: *"Redeem every firstborn son." Not sacrifice. Redeem.*

Israel's firstborns are symbolically claimed, then returned. The meaning is deliverance, not death: the firstborns were spared in Egypt, and the consecration becomes a memorial that life is preserved by mercy.

Pagan logic: "Give your child to save yourself."

Biblical logic: "Your child lives because I saved you."

What about Jesus — wasn't that human sacrifice?

Not in the pagan sense. In paganism, humans offer children to appease gods. In Christianity, *God gives Himself* for humanity. The direction is reversed. The cross is not humans feeding divine violence; it is divine self-giving absorbing human violence.

Conclusion

God never required human sacrifice — not a firstborn son, not anyone. Sacrifices were a temporary pedagogy: confronting sin, restraining brutality, rejecting pagan cruelty, and preparing humanity for the Gospel's most radical reversal:

God does not demand your child.

God gives His own.

And that reversal is one of Scripture's clearest moral signatures.

***

Q 17. Why did God destroy Sodom and Gomorrah, including children?

The Bible does not present the destruction of Sodom and Gomorrah as impulsive, indiscriminate violence. It presents it as judgment after prolonged moral collapse, undertaken with restraint, warning, and moral investigation — yet still tragic.

That tension is intentional.

Sodom is judged for systemic evil, not isolated sin

Sodom is often reduced to a single category of wrongdoing, but Scripture describes something broader and more disturbing: a society where violence, exploitation, and dehumanization were normalized.

The defining mark of Sodom is not merely private immorality but *public injustice:* abuse of the vulnerable, predatory violence, contempt for hospitality, collective participation in cruelty.

This was not a city with a few bad actors. It was a culture where evil had become structural.

Judgment comes only after investigation and warning

Before destruction, the biblical narrative emphasizes scrutiny, not haste. God listens to outcry. God investigates. God reveals His intention.

Abraham's dialogue with God matters here. God allows His justice to be questioned and agrees that *if even a small number of righteous people were present, the city would be spared.*

That exchange exists to show this: judgment is not arbitrary.

Why were children included?

This is the most painful part — and the Bible does not soften it. Scripture does not say children were morally guilty in the same way as adults. Their inclusion is not framed as punishment for personal wrongdoing. Instead, the Bible confronts a tragic reality:
when collective evil reaches a certain depth, its consequences consume the innocent as well as the guilty.

This dynamic is not limited to biblical judgment narratives. We see it throughout human history whenever injustice becomes systemic — in wars, genocides, famines, and societal collapse. These tragedies are not automatically divine acts of judgment; they are the devastating outworking of human evil when it matures unchecked.

Scripture does not romanticize this reality. It refuses to pretend that innocence insulates from fallout. Instead, it records the truth about a fractured world — and then points beyond it to redemption.

Divine judgment is not the same as human violence

Here the distinction matters. Human violence is often self-serving, disproportionate, motivated by power or fear.

Biblical judgment is portrayed as reluctant, delayed, morally constrained, final rather than cyclical. God does not benefit from destruction. Scripture repeatedly states that God takes no pleasure in death and prefers repentance to judgment.

Sodom is destroyed only after mercy is exhausted.

Why not spare the children separately?

This is where modern readers often imagine cleaner solutions than history allows.

The Bible presents judgment not as a surgical operation but as the *collapse of a moral ecosystem* that can no longer sustain life without perpetuating injustice. To preserve children inside a culture that had become irredeemably violent would not be mercy — it would be postponement of harm. That does not make the event less tragic. It explains why it is portrayed as *exceptional*, not normative.

The Bible does not leave this story standing alone

Sodom is not held up as a model for how God prefers to act. It is repeatedly cited as a *warning*, not a template. Later Scripture emphasizes God's patience, His preference for repentance, and His willingness to absorb judgment Himself rather than inflict it.

The cross reframes judgment entirely

Christian Scripture insists that God ultimately responds to evil not by destroying humanity, but by entering human violence and bearing its cost Himself.

If Sodom shows what happens when evil runs its full course, the cross shows God refusing to let that be the final word. Judgment is real — but it is not God's desire.

The sober conclusion

The destruction of Sodom and Gomorrah is not a story of divine cruelty.

It is a story of what happens when injustice becomes total and repentance is refused.

The inclusion of children is not a declaration that they were guilty; it is an acknowledgment that evil destroys indiscriminately once it is allowed to mature unchecked.

The Bible does not ask us to feel comfortable with this story. It asks us to feel warned. And it insists — again and again — that God's ultimate answer to human evil is not annihilation, but *self-giving intervention,* so that judgment need not be the final word for the world.

***

Q 18. Why was Noah's family saved in the Flood, while countless others — including children — drowned?

The Bible does not present the Flood as a moment of divine impatience or selective favoritism. It presents it as a last-resort judgment on a world that had become violently and irreversibly corrupt, paired with an act of preservation meant to keep humanity itself from disappearing. This is not a story about rewarding good people and punishing bad ones. It is a story about whether humanity would survive at all.

The Flood is described as judgment on total moral collapse

Scripture describes the pre-flood world in extreme terms: violence had become universal, corruption systemic, and the human heart "continually bent toward evil." This language is not casual — it signals a condition where evil was no longer episodic but structural, shaping every level of society.

In other words, the Flood is not triggered by isolated wrongdoing. It is triggered by a world that could no longer sustain life without perpetuating harm.

Noah is not saved because he is flawless

The Bible does not portray Noah as sinless or morally superior in every respect. He is saved because he *responds to God in trust within a world that refuses to listen at all.*

Noah's righteousness is relational, not heroic. He listens. He reacts. He builds the ark publicly over decades, functioning as a living warning long before the Flood arrives. The ark itself is an act of mercy before it is an act of judgment.

Why only Noah's family?

Because preservation requires continuity. If humanity were to continue at all, someone had to survive. The Flood is framed not as annihilation of humanity, but as reset and restraint, preventing evil from consuming everything. Saving Noah's family is not favoritism — it is the minimum necessary preservation of the human line.

The Flood narrative is not about selecting the *best* people — it is about identifying the *last remaining point where humanity is still responsive to God at all.* "Only Noah" does not mean "Noah was perfect." It means

Noah was the last place where trust had not collapsed completely.

Why not intervene earlier or differently?

The text emphasizes delay, warning, and patience. Noah's obedience unfolds over time, not overnight. The ark stands as a visible invitation long before the rain falls. Judgment comes only after the world proves unwilling to turn. At some point, preventing greater evil requires decisive action — even when every possible outcome is tragic.

Why water? Why totality?

Water in Scripture symbolizes both judgment and cleansing. The Flood is portrayed as *uncreation followed by re-creation* — a reversal meant to halt corruption from becoming permanent. This is why the Flood is followed immediately by covenant, promise, and restraint. God explicitly commits never to destroy the world in this way again.

That promise matters.

The Bible does not present the Flood as God's preferred solution

The Flood is not a pattern. It is an exception. Later Scripture consistently emphasizes God's grief over violence, His patience, and His desire to preserve rather than destroy. The Flood stands as a warning about where unchecked evil leads — not as a model for how God normally acts.

The Flood, reframed

Christian Scripture insists that God ultimately chooses to absorb judgment rather than unleash it.

If the Flood shows what happens when evil consumes everything, the cross shows God refusing to let that be the final answer — entering human violence and bearing its cost Himself.

Judgment is real. But destruction is not God's goal.

Conclusion

Noah's family was saved not because they were the only good people, but because *without preservation, humanity would have ended altogether.*

The drowning of countless others — including children — is not minimized or justified. It is presented as the tragic consequence of a world where evil had become total.

The Bible does not ask us to be comfortable with the Flood. It asks us to understand why it is never repeated. And it insists that God's final response to human corruption is not another flood — but self-giving mercy, so that judgment does not have to be the last word again.

***

Q 19. If God is love, how can divine judgment ever be justified?

Because love that never judges is not love at all — it is indifference.

The Bible does not define love as permissiveness, tolerance, or emotional warmth. It defines love as *faithful commitment to the good of the beloved,* and that good requires confrontation, resistance, and restraint of evil.

Judgment exists because love takes harm seriously

If God were love but never judged, then abuse would be morally neutral, exploitation would be inconsequential, and violence would have no final accounting. A God who simply "lets things go" is not loving toward victims. Love that refuses to name evil sides with the powerful by default.

Divine judgment is not the opposite of love; it is *love's refusal to cooperate with destruction.*

Judgment is about protection before it is about punishment

In Scripture, judgment consistently appears where harm has become entrenched and repentance refused. It functions as a boundary against escalating evil, as a restraint on injustice, and as a defense of the vulnerable. When a society — or a person — becomes a source of ongoing harm, love demands intervention. Judgment is that intervention when mercy has been rejected.

Love without judgment would erase moral meaning

If God never judged, then good and evil would collapse into preference, forgiveness would be meaningless, and justice would be cosmetic. The Bible insists that forgiveness matters because wrongdoing matters. Judgment is what gives mercy its weight.

Divine judgment is never impulsive

Scripture consistently portrays God as slow to anger, patient, warning before acting, responsive to repentance. Judgment is delayed, resisted, negotiated, and often withheld. It comes only when continued mercy would mean continued harm.

That reluctance is part of love.

Judgment is not God protecting Himself — it is God protecting creation

Human judgment is often self-serving. Divine judgment, as Scripture presents it, is not about wounded pride or threatened authority.

God does not judge because He is offended.

He judges because what He loves is being destroyed.

Love that watches destruction without intervening is negligent.

The tension, resolved

Christianity makes a claim unlike any other: God does not simply judge evil — He bears its cost Himself.

At the cross judgment is not denied; justice is not bypassed; evil is not excused. Instead, God absorbs what judgment requires rather than transferring it to others. This is the clearest statement of divine love: God does not stand apart from judgment. He steps into it.

Judgment is love's last word against evil — not its first

The Bible never celebrates judgment. It mourns it. Judgment appears when warning has failed, mercy has been refused, and harm has become irreversible.

And even then, judgment is not presented as God's desire, but as His refusal to allow evil to have the final word.

Conclusion

Divine judgment is justified not *despite* God being love, but *because He is love.*

A God who loves must oppose what destroys.

A God who loves must defend the vulnerable.

A God who loves must refuse to call evil "acceptable."

The Bible's most radical claim is not that God judges — but that He would rather suffer judgment Himself than abandon the world to it.

Love that never judges is weak.

Judgment without love is cruel.

Our God is neither.

***

Q 20. Why does God allow polygamy in Scripture while also commanding fidelity and condemning adultery?

Because Scripture makes a clear distinction between what God permits within a broken world and what He reveals as His design.

Allowance is not approval.

Narrative is not command.

From the beginning, the biblical vision of marriage is unambiguous: one man and one woman joined in covenant fidelity. That pattern appears in creation itself and is never revised. Polygamy enters the story only after humanity's fracture. It spreads through cultures shaped by survival, power imbalance, and economic vulnerability. Yet nowhere does God command it, celebrate it, or present it as ideal.

Instead, Scripture tells the truth about it.

Every polygamous household recorded in the Bible bears visible strain — jealousy between wives, favoritism among children, rivalry, manipulation, fracture, generational wounds. Abraham, Jacob, David, Solomon — their stories are not endorsements. They are cautionary accounts.

The Bible does not insert modern commentary; it lets consequences testify.

Why then regulate something that falls short of God's design?

Because God works within historical realities without sanctifying them. In ancient societies, marriage often functioned as economic protection. Widows and unmarried women could face starvation. Sudden abolition of polygamy in such conditions might have produced abandonment rather than protection. Law, therefore, restrains harm while history unfolds toward healing.

Regulation limits injustice without declaring injustice good.

Throughout Scripture, however, the direction remains consistent. Fidelity is never relaxed. Adultery is condemned because covenant exclusivity reflects God's own covenant faithfulness. Over time, revelation narrows the vision: later writings emphasize mutuality, exclusivity, and sacrificial love. Leaders are required to be "husbands of one wife." Jesus explicitly returns to creation — not culture — as the standard.

The trajectory is clear.

God permits certain distortions while patiently guiding humanity back toward the original design: faithful, exclusive, covenantal love.

***

Q 21. If all humanity comes from Adam and Eve, how is incest both unavoidable and condemned?

Because survival conditions at humanity's origin are not moral templates for mature society.

Scripture distinguishes between beginnings and boundaries.

If humanity begins with a single pair, early reproduction necessarily involves close kinship. At that stage there are no alternative populations, no extended social structures, no developed legal systems, and no generational accumulation of biological decay. It is an original condition, not a moral endorsement.

Moral prohibition arises when meaningful alternatives and predictable harm exist.

As humanity expands, complexity increases. Power imbalances become possible. Familial authority structures solidify. Genetic vulnerability accumulates. Social harm becomes foreseeable. At that point, law intervenes.

Biblical prohibitions against incest appear within a framework concerned primarily with protection — especially of the vulnerable. Incest concentrates power inside family systems in ways that foster coercion, abuse, and secrecy. Moral law addresses these dangers once they become real and preventable.

A command presupposes choice. Condemnation presumes viable alternatives.

Scripture never suggests that what was necessary for origin remains acceptable for civilization. The same developmental pattern appears elsewhere: certain behaviors are tolerated early but later restricted as society stabilizes and moral clarity sharpens.

This is not contradiction. It is moral maturation.

The Bible does not confuse survival with sanctification. It guards human dignity once human complexity makes protection essential.

***

Q 22. Why does God seem to tolerate behaviors in the Old Testament that He later condemns? Did God change?

No. God's character remains constant. What changes is humanity's capacity to receive, respond to, and live out moral truth.

Scripture consistently portrays God as just, faithful, and opposed to exploitation. Yet He engages cultures marked by violence, tribal survival, patriarchy, economic fragility, and moral confusion. He does not affirm these conditions. He restrains their worst expressions while gradually reshaping them.

Accommodation is not endorsement.

It is mercy within limitation.

Moral formation unfolds progressively. Law does not arrive all at once in its most refined form because humanity cannot bear it. Revelation deepens as hearts soften and structures stabilize.

Jesus addresses this directly. When questioned about earlier permissions, He explains that certain allowances existed because of hardness of heart — not because they reflected God's ultimate intention. Then He points back to the beginning.

That statement clarifies everything: the earlier tolerance was temporary; the original design was permanent.

Across Scripture, the trajectory never reverses. Human dignity is elevated. Violence is restrained and then condemned. Exploitative power is challenged and inverted. Covenant love becomes the model. Mercy expands without abandoning justice.

If God were inconsistent, moral direction would fluctuate. Instead, it steadily intensifies toward sacrificial love.

The Old Testament does not sanitize human behavior. It records it. Many troubling actions are described without being endorsed. The honesty of the narrative is part of its moral realism.

In Christ, the pattern reaches clarity. God does not merely issue higher standards — He fulfills them. What was once regulated externally becomes transformed internally. Justice is not relaxed; it is absorbed.

God does not revise His morality.

He patiently raises humanity toward it.

Pause. Reflect. Stand honestly before God.

• When confronted with difficult passages, is the impulse to judge God's character — or to examine assumptions about justice and love?

• Do I expect divine action to mirror modern instincts — or do I allow Scripture to define holiness on its own terms?

• When reading about judgment, does discomfort come from compassion for the innocent — or resistance to accountability?

• If love never confronts harm, would that still be love?

• Where in my life has patience been mistaken for weakness — or restraint mistaken for approval?

• When mercy delays judgment in my own life, is it received with humility — or presumed upon?

• Do I prefer a God who never judges — or a God who ultimately sets things right?

• When Scripture reveals moral development across history, does that feel like inconsistency — or patience?

• Is the desire for simpler answers stronger than the willingness to sit under divine authority?

• If God is holy love, what in me resists that holiness more than that love?

About Evil, Suffering & Pain

Q 23. Why does God allow evil at all? If He is all-powerful, why not stop it?

Because a world capable of love, responsibility, courage, and trust must also be a world where those realities can be rejected.

Freedom is not decorative. It is structural.

Evil is not a separate substance God could simply delete. It is the distortion of good capacities — will turned selfish, power turned violent, desire turned exploitative. To eliminate all evil instantly, God would have to override human intention at its source. But once intention is overridden, moral agency disappears. And without moral agency, love becomes programming.

A world where no one can choose wrong is also a world where no one can meaningfully choose right.

We often imagine a middle option: "Why not prevent only the worst evils?" But evil does not arrive cleanly labeled. It grows through thought, desire, silence, fear, ideology, habit, complicity. Where would intervention begin? At the first violent impulse? At the spoken word? At the cultural system that nurtures it?

Scripture presents a different claim: God allows evil temporarily because He intends not merely to suppress it, but to defeat it without annihilating those still capable of repentance.

Immediate eradication of evil would mean immediate eradication of every will still resisting God — and that includes more of humanity than we are comfortable admitting.

God's patience is not tolerance of evil. It is space for transformation.

And Christianity makes a claim no philosophy dares to make: God does not permit evil from a distance. He enters it. He absorbs betrayal, injustice, violence, humiliation, and death. The cross is not an explanation of evil. It is God taking responsibility for its cost.

A deity who remained untouched could be accused of indifference. A God who suffers cannot.

Why, then, does He not end evil now?

Because judgment ends history. And history continues because mercy continues.

Evil is allowed for a time. It is not allowed forever. Scripture insists that it has reach, but not sovereignty; influence, but not final authority.

The Bible does not promise a world without evil yet.

It promises a world where evil will not outlast God.

***

Q 24. Why doesn't God intervene more often — especially in cases of genocide, abuse, and injustice?

This question is not theoretical. It is visceral.

Constant intervention would not simply interrupt atrocities — it would dissolve the moral structure of human existence.

To prevent genocide, abuse, or systemic injustice at the moment of action, God would have to override human will long before violence manifests. He would need to neutralize hatred before it matures, dismantle systems before they entrench, silence lies before they spread, disrupt ambition before it organizes.

History would cease to be a moral arena and become a controlled simulation.

No one could be accountable.

No one could meaningfully repent.

No one could genuinely choose courage over fear.

We ask for intervention at the visible explosion. But atrocities are cultivated slowly — through fear, ideology, silence, ambition, and collective compliance. Preventing the end-stage horror requires dismantling the entire network of human agency that produced it.

That would mean redesigning humanity, not rescuing it.

Scripture does not present God as passive. It presents Him as restrained. Judgment is delayed not because injustice is trivial, but because premature reckoning would eliminate the possibility of repentance, resistance, and redemption.

God intervenes when collapse becomes irreversible. But He does not intervene so frequently that humans are relieved of responsibility for one another.

And here the question becomes uncomfortable.

Much of what we demand God to stop is what He commands humanity to resist.

Injustice persists not only because God is silent — but because humans are. Christianity's most radical claim is not that God interrupts every atrocity. It is that He enters human violence and allows it to exhaust itself upon Him. The cross does not prevent every genocide. It exposes every genocide as condemned. It declares that no injustice escapes final accounting.

We often want selective justice — destruction for perpetrators, mercy for ourselves, and minimal disruption to systems that benefit us.

Divine justice is not selective.

If God intervened decisively today, many oppressors would fall — and many beneficiaries of injustice would stand exposed. Intervention is not a clean surgical act. It is celestial calculation.

Scripture promises that reckoning will come. But delay is not endorsement. It is the final window for repentance, rescue, courage, and witness.

God's silence is not consent.

It is time.

And time is not protection for evil.

It is mercy for those who still have the chance to turn.

***

Q 25. Is pain necessary? Couldn't God teach humanity without suffering?

Pain was not part of humanity's original design.

In Scripture, God teaches through presence, relationship, and trust — not through injury. Before rupture, instruction flows from communion. Pain enters only after trust is broken. It is not a teaching strategy. It is a *consequence of fracture.*

So, the answer is not that God prefers suffering — but that once truth is resisted, pain becomes one of the few remaining ways reality can still reach us.

God can communicate information without pain. What pain addresses is not ignorance, but denial. We often know what is good. What we resist is admitting that our choices destroy ourselves and others.

When warning is ignored, consequence becomes the teacher.

Could God prevent that? Yes — by interrupting every destructive decision before it matures. But that would mean overriding human will. And once will is overridden, moral formation disappears. Love that cannot be refused is not love. Growth that cannot be resisted is not transformation.

Pain reveals what illusion conceals: that we are not self-sufficient; that our actions carry weight; that harm spreads beyond intention; and that love costs something.

Pain is not the lesson itself. It is the exposure of truth when gentler means have failed.

And Christianity adds something radical: God does not merely allow pain. He does not stand above suffering, issuing explanations. He absorbs betrayal, injustice, humiliation, and death.

The cross is not God saying, "Endure this."

It is God saying, "I am here inside it."

Pain is temporary. Restoration is final. Scripture ends not with better coping strategies, but with the removal of suffering altogether. Pain exists because love is still resisted. When love is fully restored, pain has no function left.

God did not need suffering to teach humanity. Humanity made suffering unavoidable. And rather than abandon us to it, God chose to carry it with us.

***

Q 26. Why do innocent people suffer while the wicked often prosper?

Because we are living in a morally fractured world — not a completed one.

The Bible does not promise immediate moral symmetry. It openly acknowledges the outrage: the unjust flourish, the faithful, endure loss, and the violent — accumulate influence.

This is not hidden. It is named.

Prosperity in Scripture is never treated as proof of righteousness. Wealth and influence can insulate a person from consequence, but insulation is not blessing. Often it corrodes slowly — hardening the heart, distorting perception, magnifying pride.

Apparent success is not final verdict.

The innocent suffer because evil, when allowed space, does not confine itself to its architects. Harm radiates outward. Systems built on exploitation injure those who did not build them. Violence does not ask permission from innocence before it strikes.

To prevent all innocent suffering immediately would require either erasing human freedom, dismantling every unjust structure at once, or ending history altogether.

God chooses neither annihilation nor constant override.

Scripture insists that justice delayed is not justice denied. Final reckoning is not abandoned — it is reserved. If there were no final accounting, then injustice would be permanent and suffering meaningless.

Christianity deepens the claim further: the most innocent life endured the most unjust death. That does not trivialize suffering. It declares that suffering is not evidence of abandonment.

The story is not over.

We are living in the long middle, not the end.

Prosperity is not ultimate.

Suffering is not definitive.

Judgment is not canceled.

Restoration is not imaginary.

No faithfulness is forgotten.

No injustice is permanent.

***

Q 27. If God loves us, why does He remain silent during our darkest moments?

Silence is not the same as absence.

The Bible does not conceal this experience. Its most faithful voices cry out in bewilderment: Where are You? Why do You hide? How long? Even Jesus utters the language of abandonment.

These cries are not censored. They are preserved.

That alone tells us something: God is not threatened by the accusation of silence.

There are forms of love that do not announce themselves through constant reassurance. When God speaks continuously, faith can remain shallow. When God is silent, trust becomes stripped of transaction.

Silence exposes whether we are seeking comfort — or God Himself.

God's silence is never inactivity. Often it is restraint. Preparation. Protection from answers we are not ready to bear. What feels like absence may be work occurring beyond our perception.

Silence does not mean nothing is happening.

It means something is not being explained.

God does not anesthetize pain immediately because numbness prevents deeper healing. Some truths form only in darkness. Some attachments fall away only when lesser supports fail.

And Christianity makes an astonishing claim: God knows what it is to cry out and receive no audible reply. Divine silence is not foreign to Him.

God does not always answer when we demand it.

He answers when the soul is ready to hear without illusion.

Silence is not the final word.

It is the interval before revelation.

Pause. Reflect. Stand honestly before God.

- When suffering unsettles faith, do I question God — or seek Him?

- When evil appears unchecked, is my heart demanding control — or asking what love truly requires of freedom?

- When injustice wounds me deeply, is there grief before God — or quiet alignment with comfort?

- When pain exposes fragility, do I resist what it reveals — or am open to what it uncovers?

- When darkness feels overwhelming, am I accusing God of absence — or remembering Him as the One who entered suffering Himself?

- When mercy delays judgment, is my faith shaken?

- And in the presence of pain, is the deepest desire for me a relief — or redemption?

About Tradition, Ritual & Holidays

Q 28. Is Christmas really Jesus' birthday — or just a tradition shaped by culture and convenience?

This question is difficult — not because the historical answer is complicated, but because the spiritual implications are.

Historically, December 25 is not confirmed as the date of Jesus' birth. The early church did not record or command a specific celebration of His nativity. The date emerged centuries later, shaped by cultural rhythms and ecclesiastical decisions.

But the date is not the deepest issue.

The deeper question is this: what are we actually celebrating?

I will begin with a personal testimony.

For years, I loved Christmas passionately. I decorated obsessively. I curated atmosphere. I orchestrated warmth, gifts, music, food, aesthetics — all in pursuit of something I thought I could build with enough effort: unity, joy, healing.

I wanted to create love.

I did not seek the One who is Love.

I had beautiful moments. But beneath the lights and photographs, I was exhausted, fractured, trying to manufacture what only surrender could produce. Christmas became a stage where I performed wholeness I did not possess.

Only recently did I see what I had been doing. I was trying to redeem my own fragile kingdom through sentiment, sacrifice, and control. I believed endurance could substitute for surrender. I believed atmosphere could compensate for alignment.

It could not.

The hardest decision I made in 2025 was to remove Christmas from my life — decorations, rituals, nostalgia, aesthetic attachments. Not because ornaments are inherently evil, but because in my life they have become substitutes. They comforted me more than truth confronted me.

Let me be clear: I am not declaring that all Christmas observance is idolatry.

I am confessing that mine had become so.

Scripture does not command an annual celebration of Christ's birth. It commands remembrance of His death. It commands communion. It commands obedience, repentance, daily discipleship.

When tradition comforts us without reordering us, it risks becoming replacement rather than remembrance.

Christmas is not sinful because it is December 25. It becomes spiritually dangerous when sentiment replaces submission, when coziness substitutes for consecration, and when seasonal attention replaces surrendered living.

God does not ask for an annual gesture.

He asks for a yielded life.

The date is an empty number.

Authority is the substance.

And for me, the only way to remove substitution was to remove participation.

That is my conviction.

Not my condemnation of others.

***

Q 29. Is Easter rooted in pagan traditions, and if so, why do Christians still celebrate it?

The resurrection itself is not pagan. It is the central historical claim of Christianity: that Jesus Christ was crucified and rose bodily from the dead.

But the cultural expressions surrounding Easter — fertility symbols, seasonal imagery, eggs, rabbits — did not originate from the Gospels. They emerged as cultural adaptations over time, merging spring symbolism with resurrection language.

Again, the issue is not historical borrowing alone.

It is what borrowing does to meaning

Early Christians did not hold annual resurrection pageantry. They remembered the risen Christ by breaking bread, by repentance, by radical obedience, and often by suffering. Resurrection was not a holiday — it was a *transformed existence.*

Over time, remembrance became celebration. Celebration became ritual. Ritual absorbed cultural symbolism. None of this automatically equals corruption. But something subtle can occur: the cross recedes, and spring takes its place.

The resurrection is not seasonal renewal.

It is a violent interruption of death.

It is judgment upon evil.

It is vindication through execution.

When resurrection is reduced to optimism, or rebirth imagery, or gentle uplift, something essential is softened. The scandal disappears. The cost fades. The demand lessens.

And that is where danger lies.

The resurrection does not need decoration to be meaningful. It demands participation. Scripture commands believers to remember Christ through communion — through shared suffering and shared life — not through symbolic pageantry. The earliest church did not ask how to make resurrection culturally accessible. They asked how to live as the God who died for us.

Again, I am not issuing universal prohibition.

I am naming my personal realization.

I wanted resurrection joy without crucifixion obedience. I preferred celebration to surrender. I found it easier to gather around symbolism than to confront daily dying to self.

The resurrection does not belong to a calendar. It belongs to a cross. And the cross belongs to daily life.

When celebration replaces repentance, when cultural comfort replaces costly discipleship, when symbolism becomes easier than submission — the line between remembrance and substitution blurs.

The resurrection does not require reenacting once a year. It asks to be embodied.

And that difference changed everything for me.

Pause. Reflect. Stand honestly before God.

• When a tradition feels sacred, is it drawing my heart toward obedience — or toward nostalgia?

• When certain ritual comforts me, does it also confront me?

• When remembering the birth or resurrection of Jesus, a life reordering — or merely decorating it?

• Is participating in cultural celebration, an authority coming from Scripture — or from familiarity?

- If every external expression was removed, would my devotion remain intact?

- When joy is felt, is it rooted in obedience — or in sentiment?

About Faith, Freedom & Choice

Q 30. If God wants a relationship, why does He allow doubt, distance, and ambiguity?

Because relationship requires freedom — and freedom includes the possibility of distance. If God made His presence as undeniable as gravity, belief would no longer be trust; it would be reflex. Scripture consistently shows that God does not seek forced acknowledgment but freely chosen devotion. Ambiguity is not a flaw in revelation — it is the environment in which love becomes meaningful.

Distance also reveals the heart. When God feels absent, what surfaces is not a lack of information but the orientation of desire: do we seek truth, comfort, control, or escape? The Bible shows people witnessing miracles and still resisting God. Clarity alone does not heal the will. Ambiguity exposes it.

That is why Scripture speaks of seeking, knocking, and waiting. Not because God enjoys hiding — but because relationship grows through pursuit, not possession.

Christianity makes an even deeper claim: God does not remain distant from doubt. In Christ, He steps into silence, suffering, and even the experience of abandonment. The cross is not God avoiding ambiguity; it is God entering it.

He makes Himself knowable, not unavoidable — present enough to be found, quiet enough to be refused.

***

Q 31. Why does God demand obedience — doesn't that contradict freedom?

Only if freedom is defined as self-rule.

Scripture defines freedom differently: as alignment with truth.

God does not command obedience to protect His ego or authority. He commands it because He is the source of life. To obey Him is not to shrink freedom, but to live in harmony with reality. A fish is not constrained by water; it is sustained by it. Outside it, what looks like freedom becomes suffocation.

Obedience also presupposes choice. It can be refused — and often is. Scripture records rebellion without concealment. That allowance is the cost of genuine relationship. Compelled compliance would remove defiance, but it would also remove love, responsibility, and trust.

In Christianity, obedience is not submission to distant power but response to self-giving love. The cross reframes the question. God does not demand obedience from above; He demonstrates it first — entering suffering, relinquishing power, and bearing cost.

Obedience, then, is not loss of freedom. It is liberation from the illusion that autonomy equals life.

***

Q 32. Is faith blind belief, or a form of knowing beyond reason?

Biblical faith is not blind belief. It includes reason — but does not end with it.

Blind belief accepts claims without grounding or examination. Scripture invites the opposite: reasoning, testing, wrestling, remembering. "Come, let us reason together." "Test everything." "Examine." Doubt is not forbidden; refusal to follow truth once seen **is.**

Reason asks whether something is coherent, plausible, morally intelligible. Faith asks whether we will entrust ourselves to what reason has brought into view.

Some realities cannot be reduced to proof without distortion. Love, loyalty, trust, and forgiveness cannot be measured like equations, yet they are among the most real forces in human life. Faith operates in that same relational space: it is knowledge of a Person, not just assent to propositions.

Faith is not belief without evidence. It is commitment in light of it.

Reason can bring us to the threshold.

Faith is the step that crosses it.

***

Q 33. What if I want to believe — but can't?

This question is honest — and Scripture honors honesty.

Wanting to believe but feeling unable is not the same as rejecting God. Often it means you are standing where belief would require more than agreement — it would require surrender.

The Bible distinguishes doubt from refusal. Doubt seeks understanding. Refusal avoids transformation. Jesus does not condemn those who struggle; He confronts those who close themselves off.

Faith cannot be manufactured. You cannot argue yourself into it or perform yourself into it. *It emerges when truth meets willingness.* That is why the invitation is always relational: ask, seek, knock. Not "convince yourself," but "come closer."

There is also a protective truth here: sometimes we say we want to believe while quietly setting conditions — believe, but without change; trust, but without relinquishing control. Scripture says God knows the heart more clearly than we do. Self-deception is possible. But so is breakthrough.

The Bible repeatedly shows God moving toward those who are reaching but unsure — Thomas doubting, a father crying "Help my unbelief," (Mark 9:24), Saul blinded before he sees. God is not threatened by your inability. What He resists is indifference.

If you want to believe but cannot, stop trying to force certainty. Instead, pursue God honestly. Ask what stands in the way — fear, pride, hurt, misrepresentation. Stay present.

Faith often arrives quietly — not as arguments that you won, but as recognition dawning.

And Scripture promises this without exception: Those who truly seek will be found — not because they were strong enough to believe, but because God is faithful enough to meet them.

***

Q 34. What if I believe — but I'm angry at God?

Belief and anger are not opposites. In Scripture, they often coexist.

The Psalms protest. Job argues. Prophets accuse. These voices are not erased; they are canonized. Anger spoken to God is still relationship. What Scripture warns against is not protest — but withdrawal.

Anger usually arises from wounded trust. We are rarely angry at someone we do not care about. If you are angry at God, it likely means you believed something about His goodness that now feels contradicted. Scripture treats this not as automatic rebellion, but as grief demanding articulation.

The crucial distinction is this: Anger expressed can become prayer. Anger suppressed becomes bitterness.

Bring it to Him. Name what feels unjust. Speak what feels unfair. Faith does not require emotional polish; it requires truthfulness.

Christianity makes a profound claim here: God is not untouched by human anguish. In Christ, He cries out in abandonment. That cry does not signal disbelief — it reveals the depth of trust that continues even when feeling collapses.

If you believe and are angry, remain in conversation. Stay present. Refuse to sever the relationship. Trust rebuilt after anger is often deeper than trust never tested.

God is not afraid of your anger.

He is concerned only that you bring it to Him rather than away from Him.

Pause. Reflect. Stand honestly before God.

• When doubt surfaces, does it lead me toward seeking — or toward retreat?

• Is faith an agreement for me — or surrender?

• When belief feels difficult, what I am protecting — reputation, control, comfort?

• When anger rises toward God, am I bringing it into prayer — or am I allowing it to harden into distance?

• When standing before God, is my heart seeking validation — or transformation?

About Meaning, Identity & Hope

Q 35. What is the purpose of suffering if it does not lead to healing?

This question assumes healing is the only legitimate outcome of suffering. Scripture quietly rejects that assumption.

Suffering does not justify itself through results. It is not a tidy lesson or an efficient tool. Much pain does not restore what was lost. Job's children are not returned. Many psalms close without answers. Jesus heals many — but not all — and offers no universal explanation.

If suffering has purpose, it cannot be reduced to visible resolution. It must be understood in terms of truth.

One purpose of suffering is revelation. Pain exposes what comfort conceals — our misplaced trusts, fragile illusions, and unexamined loyalties. It strips away pretense. This exposure is not therapeutic in the modern sense, but it is clarifying. Even when nothing is repaired, something false is often removed.

Another purpose is witness. Not all suffering heals the sufferer — but some suffering bears testimony. The prophets endure rejection. The apostles endure persecution. Christ endures the cross. Their pain is not redeemed by personal relief, but by what it reveals: injustice named, evil unmasked, faithfulness made visible.

Most unsettling of all, Scripture suggests that suffering may remain unresolved and still not be meaningless. *God's answer to suffering is not explanation but presence.* In Christ, He does not justify pain from afar; He enters it.

So, if suffering does not lead to healing, its purpose is not punishment or improvement. Its purpose may be this: to remain truthful in a fractured world until redemption comes. Not all suffering makes us stronger. Some suffering simply makes us honest.

That is not comforting.

But it is faithful.

***

Q 36. Does pain have meaning—or do we simply assign meaning to survive it?

The answer depends on what kind of world we believe we inhabit.

If reality is impersonal, then pain has no inherent meaning. It happens, and we construct narratives to endure it. Meaning becomes adaptive, not true. This explains coping — but not justice.

Scripture offers a more demanding claim: pain exists within a moral universe. That does not mean every instance has a decipherable purpose. The Bible rejects that simplification. Job receives no explanation. Jesus refuses to equate suffering with guilt. Meaning is not a tidy answer.

But meaning is not invented either.

Pain exposes injustice. It reveals the cost of love. It confronts denial. Its meaning is not always why it occurs, but what it uncovers — about the world, about us, about God.

Christianity grounds this claim in a startling assertion: God entered suffering. The cross does not explain pain away; it anchors it in divine solidarity. Meaning is not something we fabricate to endure. It is something we encounter when pain strips away illusion and leaves us face-to-face with truth.

Pain does not always heal.

But it does not lie.

***

Q 37. What does it mean to be saved — from what, and for what?

To ask what salvation means is to ask whether something is truly broken — and whether it can be restored.

In Scripture, salvation is not a rescue from discomfort or mortality. It is a rescue from rupture. Sin is not merely rule-breaking; it is relational fracture — a turning from the source of life. To be saved is to be reconciled.

Saved from what?

From self-enclosure. From guilt that effort cannot undo. From death — not only as a future event, but as a present force that erodes trust, meaning, and love. Salvation addresses the root, not merely the symptoms.

Saved for what?

For restored belonging and renewed purpose. Salvation is not a private escape plan; it is reorientation. It is being drawn back into communion — with God, with truth, with a story larger than survival. It frees us into obedience, not from responsibility.

Christianity insists that salvation is received, not achieved. It is not self-improvement but surrender. And it does not end in personal peace. It moves outward — into witness, endurance, and costly love.

To be saved is not simply to be spared from judgment.

It is to be reclaimed for life as it was always meant to be lived.

***

Q 38. If God already knows everything, does my choice really matter?

Yes.

Divine knowledge does not cancel human freedom. Knowing a choice is not the same as causing it. Scripture never equates foreknowledge with coercion.

God's knowing transcends time; it does not manipulate it. He does not wait to learn what you will do — but neither does He force you to do it. His knowledge encompasses your freedom without erasing it.

The Bible treats choice as morally consequential precisely because it can be refused. Commands, warnings, invitations, and consequences would be meaningless if agency were an illusion. God pleads, grieves, and rejoices in response to human decisions. That language would be hollow if freedom were theatrical.

Most strikingly, Christianity claims that God enters the consequences of human freedom. In Christ, He absorbs rejection, violence, betrayal. If choices were insignificant, the cross would be unnecessary.

Your decisions matter not because they surprise God, but because

He has chosen to let them shape real history. Love does not negate freedom. Knowledge does not eliminate responsibility.

God knows the end.

But He meets us in the choosing.

***

Q 39. Is redemption possible for people who feel irreparably broken?

Yes.

Not because they are less damaged than they believe — but because brokenness is not the barrier Scripture identifies.

Redemption does not begin where wholeness remains. It begins where self-repair fails. The Bible consistently portrays God choosing the compromised, the ashamed, the exhausted. Moses is reluctant. David is morally fractured. Peter denies. Paul persecutes. None are restored before being redeemed.

Redemption does not mean returning to who you were before the damage. It means being transformed into something that could not exist without it.

The resurrection preserves Christ's wounds. They are not erased; they are glorified. That detail is not incidental. It signals that scars are not disqualifying. They can become part of truth.

What blocks redemption is rarely the depth of harm. It is the belief that one must first become worthy of restoration. Scripture dismantles that logic. Redemption is not earned by readiness or strength. It is received through surrender.

For those who feel beyond repair, Christianity does not promise instant healing or tidy outcomes. It promises that nothing true about you lies outside God's reach, and nothing false must be defended.

Redemption may not feel like relief. It may feel like being seen fully — and not rejected there. That is not optimism. It is the logic of the cross.

If redemption were reserved for the repairable, no one would qualify.

The gospel exists precisely because irreparable brokenness is what God knows how to meet.

Pause. Reflect. Stand honestly before God.

- When a pain I carry does not heal, do I dismiss it as meaningless — or am I allowing it to reveal what is true?

- When my pain strips away illusions, is truth welcomed — or resisted?

- When my identity feels fractured, is it defined by wounds — or by what God declares?

- When I think about salvation, do I see it as escape — or restoration?

• When I make choices, are they treated as temporary — or eternal in weight?

• When prosperity surrounds the unjust, does my hope shift — or remain anchored in God's justice?

• Restoration requires surrender, not self-repair. What would I need to release?

Appendix II

The Lion and the Lamb — Songs by Ashes of Light

Before this book was written, these songs were born.

They were not composed as commentary, but as cry.

Not argument, but confession.

Not explanation, but encounter.

The Lion and the Lamb is not a soundtrack to these pages — it is their condensed form.

Each song carries the same themes explored in prose: pain, judgment, redemption, surrender, resurrection, identity, and the battle between illusion and truth.

If the chapters reason, the songs testify.

If the essays analyze, the songs bleed.

They are not meant to persuade.

They are meant to echo.

You may read them as poetry.

You may scan the QR codes and listen.

But most of all, read them slowly — as prayers set to fire.

Scan to listen to the entire album on Spotify

Watch the videos

The Prophecy

And the One Who IS spoke — 'Let there be light,'
And the void split apart, pierced by His might
The darkness trembled, and waters appeared
The stars, the land, the Life in His palm
And the gentle Spirit, roaming near
And eternal, peaceful, beautiful psalm

Despised and rejected, and broken to pieces,
covered in blood, with a crown of thorns.
He bore the Cross, wishing no pity,
But only to be His Father's Son.

The heavens will burn, the mountains will fall,
The trumpet will sound, the nations will call.
The day is at hand, the dark will take flight,
The King will return in His power and might!

I saw the fire that poured from His gaze,
The earth stood trembling, curled in His hands
The stars fell down like a storm from the sky,
The proud men knelt before the Lord's might.

A voice like waters broke through the air,
"Stand, child of dust, for the hour is near.
The armies of shadow are drawing their line,
But victory's coming, the battle is Mine!"

Despised and rejected, and broken to pieces,
covered in blood, with a crown of thorns.
He bore the Cross, wishing no pity,
But only to be His Father's Son

The heavens will burn, the mountains will fall,

The trumpet will sound, the nations will call.
The day is at hand, the dark will take flight,
The King will return in His power and might!

"The scroll will open, the seals will break,
The earth will tremble, the dead will awake.
The gates of brass will shatter in flame,
The world will bow to His holy name."

The heavens will burn, the mountains will fall,
The trumpet will sound, the nations will call.
The day is at hand, the dark will take flight,
The King will return in His power and might!

"Choose your side... for the hour has come."

Watch the official video

The Fool Behind the Mask

All my life I've juggled with sorrow,
Dancing with pain in the howling night.
I've bargained with death for one more tomorrow,
But the noose of the lies always pulled me in tight.

I am the fool behind the mask,
A shadow no one sees.
A painted smile, a hollow laugh,
Chained by cruel decrees.
The world applauds but never knows
The cracks in what I wear—
The fool behind the mask is bleeding,
And no one really cares.

I was a friend, a voice for the broken,
A keeper of secrets they threw to the dirt.
They crowned me a fool, their jester unspoken,
But never the one they would hold when it hurt.

Carnival colors can't hide the fractures,
The truth burns deep in my eyes.
The crowd turns away, the laughter dies,
And my stage becomes my disguise.

I am the fool behind the mask,
A shadow no one sees.
A painted smile, a hollow laugh,
Chained by cruel decrees.
The world applauds but never knows
The cracks in what I wear—
The fool behind the mask is bleeding,
And no one really cares.

And in the void of the spotlight fading,
I dream of the wind calling my name.
But fate drags me back for another encore,
A hundred times… the same.

I am the fool behind the mask,
A shadow fading fast.
But the Lion called my name,
He tore the chains, the lies, the shame.
He wrapped me in His holy grace,
A love the world can't quite embrace.
The fool behind the mask is dying—
And the child of God is rising.

Watch the official video

Prey to Time

A prey to time, the clock unwinds,
Fate let down her silver hair,
Reaching deep to touch the self within,
Where shadows dance, and echoes spin.
Chains clanged deep in shadow's den,
From the stillness rose the voice of Grief,
A mournful sigh, a desperate plea,
In the barren demons' eyes, there's no reprieve.

Oh, the trumpets wail, far away they sound,
For Pride and Glory, long derailed,
And Honor, bruised, left all alone,
Curled beneath broken stone, where dreams have blown.

The solemn trio—Grief, Anger, Dread,
Their boots, they stomped, out Desire's flame,
And Fear, unbridled, staked its claim,
With every step, the darkness spread.
Faith's face grew wrinkled, bent with care,
Stars dimmed quietly in the air,
As Golgotha burned in sacred flame,
Where Beauty, Laughter, Dreams were slain.

Underneath the mud of memories lost,
In time that no longer counts the cost,
With lips cracked red from prayers alone,
God holds the world, praying to atone.
To stop this sin, this endless strife,
In the wretched game we call our life.

Light dwindles fast, but I still seek,
A whisper of courage in the meek.
In the shadow of sorrow, we stand tall,

With heavy hearts, we still hear the call.
Each haunting note resounds our fate,
We rise together, even through the hate.

Hear the voice of those who fought and lost,
Echoing through halls, reminding us of costs.
In the darkest corners of the human soul,
Where desperation rages, we must be whole.
Through the depths of despair, we'll break the chains,
With love as our armor, end all the pains.

Oh, the trumpets wail, far away they sound,
For Pride and Glory, long derailed,
And Honor, bruised, left all alone,
Curled beneath broken stone, where dreams have blown.
So gather the ashes, and rise from the dust,
With hearts ignited, we place our trust.
In the midst of the chaos, let love be our guide,
For even in darkness, there's light to confide.
As we journey through time, together we gleam,
A prey no longer, we'll weave our dream.

Watch the official video

Shadows and Redemption

In the silence of the night, I cast my gaze low,
Lowered the blinds, summoned the darkness to grow.
A womb of warmth, yet the chill cuts deep
In the muted echoes, I search for sleep.

Primal silence wraps around my soul,
In this cocoon, I've lost control.
I prayed for forgiveness, surrendered my pride,
The proud and unyielding, now here I bide.
Trees outside weep, their bark mourns the pain,
As I knelt in regret, yearning to explain.
The sins of my life weigh heavily still,
Yet in this darkness, I seek a will.

I am alone, yet I'm not afraid,
For every shadow holds the light that stayed
Behind these blinds, in sorrow bestowed,
A sacred grace, in silence flowed.

From the depths of eternity, a violin cries,
Mourning with the street dogs beneath the gray skies.
Outside, the world rages, the fruit of the womb,
Foretelling a winter, a season of gloom.
But through the fractures of this painful night,
I sense a whisper, a flicker of light.
In the distance, a soft voice breathes,
"Fear not, dear child, for love never leaves.

Through the name of Jesus, I find my peace,
His grace lifts the burden; my sorrows cease.
With every note that the violin plays,
Redemption blooms in the darkest of days.
The shadows retreat, replaced by the dawn,

As I rise from my knees, rebirth has begun.
I am alone, yet I'm not afraid,
For every shadow holds the light that stayed.
Behind these blinds, in sorrow bestowed,
A sacred grace, in silence flowed.
All the broken pieces of my former life,
He mends with love, cuts through the strife.
The silence transforms, a tranquil embrace,
I once was lost; now I'm shown grace.
I feel the warmth of forgiveness ignite,
In the raw and the ethereal, I rejoice in His light.
The trees now whisper of hope and rebirth,
Winter retreats to reveal my worth

So I lower the blinds and let daylight in,
No longer shackled by the weight of my sin.
With the sound of redemption, I rise from the floor,
In the arms of His love, I am whole evermore.
In shadows replaced, I sing my refrain,
For God's grace is wild, unbound by the pain.

Watch the official video

Through His Eyes

Every night, it's the same old wave:
Helpless ghosts I can't save.
Blood on my hands that won't wash clean,
Faces I lost… they still haunt my dreams.
I've learned to smile with a broken mouth,
Numb inside, slowly bleeding out.
And every mirror just spits my shame:
I am a scared soul, no worth the chance…

But somewhere past the smoke and flame,
I hear Him call my name…

Through His eyes, I'm not the sum of my mistakes,
Through His eyes, every chain of the past will break.
He sees a fighter when I see a ghost,
He loves the man I hate the most.
Through His eyes, I'm not defined by the pain—
Through His eyes… I'm whole again.

I was the prodigal drowning in vain
A dog returning to the same old chains.
But He tore the night with a bleeding crown,
Pulled me up when the world dragged me down.
He took my rage, turned it into light,
Gave me the will to stand and fight.
I'm more than the war that carved my skin,
I'm the soul He refused to give in.

I am the soldier, I am the child,
I am the lost one He reconciled.
I am the wreckage He built into stone,
I'm the wretched man He calls His own.

Through His eyes, I'm not the sum of my scars,
Through His eyes, I'm worth the nails and the crossbars.
He sees a victory in every tear,
He's been beside me through every fear.
Through His eyes, I'll never be the same—
Through His eyes… He loves my name.

Watch the official video

Unshakable

(A Survivor's Anthem of Redemption)
"The Lord is close to the brokenhearted… and saves those crushed in spirit."
Yeah… that was me.
The night was burning red,
Your shadow over me.
Every bruise told a story
No one dared to see.
You said you loved me,
You swore I deserved it…
That my words had provoked you,
That my silence had earned it.

Your fist was the breeze before the storm,
A kiss before the hurricane of pain.
Our sons were crying, their voices tore the air,
I reached for them… but my soul wasn't there.

I lay on the floor, cold and alone,
My eyelids heavy, shutting out the dawn.
Your voice was fading, a ghost in the dark—
You whispered, "I'm sorry… this time I'll restart."

Then you were gone… I begged you to stay,
But the silence wrapped tight, and carried me away.
And in the stillness, where hope felt slain,
A whisper broke through the weight of pain:
"For ashes, I'll give you a crown that will shine,
And call you My daughter—you're forever Mine."

I felt the chains crash down,
Felt my lungs begin to breathe.
The Lord reached into my darkness,
And He pulled me to my feet.

I am UNSHAKABLE, I am UNBROKEN,
By the hands that bled when His love was spoken.
The old has died, the new has begun,
I rise in the light of the Risen Son.

The mirror doesn't haunt me now,
The lies have lost their voice.
I stand tall, unashamed,
Because in Christ, I've made my choice.
My scars tell the truth of the hell I survived,
But they shine with the proof that my soul's alive.
His hand on my shoulder, His gaze in my eyes—
He is my freedom, my hope, my prize.

He heals the brokenhearted, binds up their wounds,
Holds my head above the flood,
Walks me past the tombs.
I'm upheld by His righteous hand,
A daughter of the King… and here I stand.

I am UNSHAKABLE, I am UNBROKEN,
My life restored by the Word He's spoken.
No night too dark, no chain too strong,
In Christ, through love, I am reborn!

"The old has gone… the new is here."
And HE… HE will always be near!

Watch the official video

Lion's Roar

I have walked through fire, felt the enemy's breath,
His whispers cling to me, chains of bitter death.
Lies etched deep in my bones, haunting every step,
In the shadows of my soul, where my demons crept.

Be strong in the Lord, let His power ignite,
Dress in the armor, prepared for the fight.
Not just flesh and blood, it's deeper than that,
Against the darkness, I will not fall flat

The enemy roars, but I feel the ground shake,
The Lion of Judah, a force none can break.
The light is coming, breaking through the night,
I will rise to meet it, I will join the fight.

On the battlefield of shadows, I search for the truth,
In the chaos of the lies, reclaiming my youth.
With every breath, I feel the weight of despair,
But I gather my strength; I will not be scared.

Gird your waist with truth, let it be your guide,
Wear the breastplate, righteousness by your side.
With the shield of faith, I'll block every dart,
The enemy's whispers, I'll tear them apart

The enemy roars, but I feel the ground shake,
The Lion of Judah, a force none can break.
The light is coming, breaking through the night,
I will rise to meet it, I will join the fight.

Take the helmet of salvation, protect your head
The sword of the Spirit, by His Word I'm led.

Stand tall, soldier of Christ, in the heat of the fire,
The Lion has roared, we'll rise even higher!

Chains are falling, doubts are breaking,
In the depths of despair, my heart is awaking.
From ashes I'll rise, like the phoenix in flight,
With faith as my armor, I'll step into the light.

The enemy roars, but I feel the ground shake,
The Lion of Judah, a force none can break.
The light is coming, breaking through the night,
I will rise to meet it, I will join the fight.

So stand your ground, when the darkness descends,
With armor in place, our battle transcends.
I've walked through the fire, but now I am free,
For in Christ, I am strong, and He fights for me!
The Lion has roared, and the Lamb has won,
Together we stand, and the battle's begun!

Watch the official video

I Am Made New

I've been watching myself bleed in the silence,
Feeding the fear that stalks in the night.
Every prayer I've cried felt like ashes,
And I ask, *where's my God in this fight?*

But He was there when the storm split the heavens,
He was there when the shadows drew near.
Devil, you can bind me in chains, but forever
You can't silence the voice that I hear.

You will break me? — I will rise.
You will take me? — Through His eyes.
Fire or light, chains or crown,
Jesus will never let me down.

The devil can promise me kingdoms and glory,
The whole world lying at my feet…
But to kneel in his dark shadow for even a moment
Would make every dream taste like defeat.
So, I'll refuse the mountains of riches and the power,
For My Lord's truth is my sword and my shield.
No crown forged in darkness can hold me,
By Jesus' name, I will never yield.

You will break me? — I will rise.
You will take me? — Through His eyes.
Fire or light, chains or crown,
Jesus will never let me down.

There's a line in the sand, and I'll cross it,
Every whisper of doubt burned away.
From the ashes I'll rise even higher,
In God's light, I will stand and stay.

You will break me? — I will rise.
You will take me? — Through His eyes.
Fire or light, chains or crown,
Jesus will never let me down.

The darkness of this world fades into His dawn,
The void I created is gone.
Chains are shattered, the light breaks through—
The battle's won, and I'm made new!

Watch the official video

Aniko, My Tiny Firefly

Silence tears me apart, like a dream left behind,
Sounds embed themselves in my flesh, eternally blind.
Craving the echoes, they carve craters in my veins,
In the ether of mute space, I'm lost in the chains
Where shadows play tricks on the thoughts that I weave,
I search for the light, for the hope I believe.

And there you are, my tiny firefly,
A flicker of warmth in the shadows of sky.
You grab my hand, whisper soft and serene,
Sit by the stream, where the world's evergreen.
Laugh with the voices of crickets at play,
Skipping barefoot in magic, we drift far away.

In a tear, like in crystal, I carve your name,
Fragile and tender, like the softest flame.
I shelter it in whispers, let it dance in the air,
Warming me with your tenderness, a love beyond compare.
Through the tattered fragments of the darkening night,
You're my beacon, my guide, leading me to the light.

And there you are, my tiny firefly,
A flicker of warmth in the shadows of sky.
You grab my hand, whisper soft and serene,
Sit by the stream, where the world's evergreen.
Laugh with the voices of crickets at play,
Skipping barefoot in magic, we drift far away

I will carry you to the ends of the earth,
Where beauty resides, where we can re-birth.
On the left, where dreams meet the blissful sunrise,
In your eyes, sweet reflections, our love never dies.
And when silence betrays, when echoes depart

Know your spirit will always reside in my heart.

In the silence, in the tears, I'll weave through the dark,
With you by my side, you forever ignite a spark.
Tiny firefly, in shadows you'll stay,
Guiding my soul as we dance in the gray.
With laughter of crickets, and streams that run free,
Together we'll blossom, just you and me.

Watch the official video

A Final Word to the Reader

The answers provided in this book are not meant to silence your questions. They are meant to give them ground sturdy enough to stand on.

Faith does not require you to stop thinking. It asks you to think honestly, to follow truth without flinching, and to allow it to confront you where it becomes costly.

Is faith opposed to reason?

No. Faith begins where reason has done its work and invites you to entrust yourself to what you have recognized as true. Reason examines. Faith commits.

God is not threatened by sincere questions. Scripture preserves the voices of doubters, protestors, and seekers because truth does not fear scrutiny. What God resists is not inquiry — but self-sufficiency. Not wrestling — but indifference.

If you are asking with humility, you are not far from truth. If you are wrestling honestly, you are not outside of faith. The distance between doubt and belief is often smaller than pride would like to admit.

Keep seeking. Keep knocking. Stay truthful.

You may discover that the One you are searching for has been nearer than you imagined.

APPENDIX III

Core References (Foundational Works)

These works form the intellectual and theological backbone of the book. They are cited not as proof-texts, but as conversation partners — voices that wrestle honestly with suffering, truth, freedom, and redemption.

A. Scripture & Theological Framework

- **The Holy Bible.** New International Version. Grand Rapids, MI: Zondervan, 2011.
- Bonhoeffer, Dietrich. The Cost of Discipleship. New York: Touchstone, 1995.
- Moltmann, Jürgen. The Crucified God. Minneapolis: Fortress Press, 1993.
- Wright, N. T. The Day the Revolution Began. New York: HarperOne, 2016.
- Barth, Karl. Church Dogmatics, Vol. IV: The Doctrine of Reconciliation. Edinburgh: T&T Clark, 1956.

B. Pain, Suffering, and Meaning

- Frankl, Viktor E. Man's Search for Meaning. Boston: Beacon Press, 2006.
- Lewis, C. S. The Problem of Pain. New York: HarperOne, 2001.
- Lewis, C. S. A Grief Observed. New York: HarperOne, 2001.
- Keller, Timothy. Walking with God through Pain and Suffering. New York: Dutton, 2013.
- Hart, David Bentley. The Doors of the Sea. Grand Rapids: Eerdmans, 2005.

C. Trauma, Memory, and the Human Body

- van der Kolk, Bessel. The Body Keeps the Score. New York: Viking, 2014.
- Herman, Judith Lewis. Trauma and Recovery. New York: Basic Books, 1992.
- Janoff-Bulman, Ronnie. Shattered Assumptions. New York: Free Press, 1992.

D. Truth, Identity, and Moral Authority

- Taylor, Charles. A Secular Age. Cambridge, MA: Belknap Press, 2007.
- MacIntyre, Alasdair. After Virtue. 3rd ed. Notre Dame, IN: University of Notre Dame Press, 2007.
- Smith, James K. A. Desiring the Kingdom. Grand Rapids: Baker Academic, 2009.

E. Freedom, Evil, and Responsibility

- Plantinga, Alvin. God, Freedom, and Evil. Grand Rapids: Eerdmans, 1974.
- Augustine. Confessions. Translated by Henry Chadwick. Oxford: Oxford University Press, 2008.
- Boethius. The Consolation of Philosophy. Translated by Victor Watts. London: Penguin Classics, 1999.

F. Witness, Martyrdom, and Redemption

- Foxe, John. Foxe's Book of Martyrs. Grand Rapids: Revell, 1981.
- Nouwen, Henri J. M. The Wounded Healer. New York: Image Books, 1979.

APPENDIX IV

Extended Scholarly & Historical References

The following sources support the historical claims, theological arguments, trauma analysis, and ethical reasoning presented throughout the book and Appendix I. They are included in full to ensure transparency, scholarly accountability, and intellectual honesty.

I. Biblical Texts and Core Theology

The Holy Bible. New International Version. Grand Rapids, MI: Zondervan, 2011.

Augustine. Confessions. Translated by Henry Chadwick. Oxford: Oxford University Press, 2008.

Augustine. The City of God. Translated by Henry Bettenson. London: Penguin Classics, 2003.

Augustine. On Free Choice of the Will. Translated by Thomas Williams. Indianapolis: Hackett, 1993.

Aquinas, Thomas. Summa Theologiae. Translated by the Fathers of the English Dominican Province. New York: Benziger Bros., 1947.

Barth, Karl. Church Dogmatics, Vol. IV: The Doctrine of Reconciliation. Edinburgh: T&T Clark, 1956.

Bonhoeffer, Dietrich. The Cost of Discipleship. New York: Touchstone, 1995.

Bonhoeffer, Dietrich. Letters and Papers from Prison. Edited by Eberhard Bethge. New York: Touchstone, 1997.

Brueggemann, Walter. Genesis. Interpretation Commentary. Atlanta: John Knox Press, 1982.

Brueggemann, Walter. The Message of the Psalms: A Theological Commentary. Minneapolis: Augsburg Fortress, 1984.

Goldingay, John. Old Testament Theology. 3 vols. Downers Grove, IL: InterVarsity Press, 2003–2009.

Moltmann, Jürgen. The Crucified God: The Cross of Christ as the Foundation and Criticism of Christian Theology. Translated by R. A. Wilson and John Bowden. Minneapolis: Fortress Press, 1993.

Stott, John R. W. The Cross of Christ. Downers Grove, IL: InterVarsity Press, 1986.

Wright, N. T. Scripture and the Authority of God. Rev. ed. New York: HarperOne, 2013.

Wright, N. T. The Day the Revolution Began. New York: HarperOne, 2016.

II. Biblical Interpretation, Canon, and Textual Transmission

Bruce, F. F. The Canon of Scripture. Downers Grove, IL: InterVarsity Press, 1988.

Bruce, F. F. Jesus and Christian Origins Outside the New Testament. Grand Rapids, MI: Eerdmans, 1974.

Ehrman, Bart D. Lost Christianities. New York: Oxford University Press, 2003.

Ehrman, Bart D. The New Testament: A Historical Introduction to the Early Christian Writings. 6th ed. New York: Oxford University Press, 2016.

Metzger, Bruce M., and Bart D. Ehrman. The Text of the New Testament: Its Transmission, Corruption, and Restoration. 4th ed. Oxford: Oxford University Press, 2005.

Tov, Emanuel. Textual Criticism of the Hebrew Bible. 3rd ed. Minneapolis: Fortress Press, 2012.

VanderKam, James C., and Peter Flint. The Meaning of the Dead Sea Scrolls.

New York: HarperCollins, 2002.

III. Jesus in History & Comparative Religion

Tacitus. The Annals. Translated by A. J. Woodman. New York: Penguin Classics, 2004.

Josephus, Flavius. The Antiquities of the Jews. Translated by William Whiston. Peabody, MA: Hendrickson, 1987.

Pliny the Younger. Letters. Translated by Betty Radice. Cambridge, MA: Harvard University Press, 1969.

Lucian of Samosata. The Death of Peregrine and Other Works. Translated by Lionel Casson. Oxford: Oxford University Press, 1993.

Sanders, E. P. The Historical Figure of Jesus. London: Penguin Books, 1993.

Van Voorst, Robert E. Jesus Outside the New Testament. Grand Rapids, MI: Eerdmans, 2000.

The Qur'an. Translated by M. A. S. Abdel Haleem. Oxford: Oxford University Press, 2005.

Parrinder, Geoffrey. Jesus in the Qur'an. Oxford: Oneworld Publications, 1995.

Smith, Huston. The World's Religions. New York: HarperOne, 1991.

IV. Evil, Suffering, Divine Hiddenness

Plantinga, Alvin. God, Freedom, and Evil. Grand Rapids: Eerdmans, 1974.

Hick, John. Evil and the God of Love. Rev. ed. London: Palgrave Macmillan, 2010.

Mackie, J. L. "Evil and Omnipotence." Mind 64, no. 254 (1955): 200–212.

Rowe, William L. "The Problem of Evil and Some Varieties of Atheism." American Philosophical Quarterly 16, no. 4 (1979): 335–341.

Schellenberg, J. L. Divine Hiddenness and Human Reason. Ithaca, NY: Cornell University Press, 1993.

Hart, David Bentley. The Doors of the Sea. Grand Rapids: Eerdmans, 2005.

Lewis, C. S. The Problem of Pain. New York: HarperOne, 2001.

Lewis, C. S. A Grief Observed. New York: HarperOne, 2001.

V. Trauma, Memory, and the Body

Herman, Judith Lewis. Trauma and Recovery. New York: Basic Books, 1992.

van der Kolk, Bessel. The Body Keeps the Score. New York: Viking, 2014.

Janoff-Bulman, Ronnie. Shattered Assumptions. New York: Free Press, 1992.

Alexander, Jeffrey C., et al. Cultural Trauma and Collective Identity. Berkeley: University of California Press, 2004.

Assmann, Jan. Cultural Memory and Early Civilization. Cambridge: Cambridge University Press, 2011.

Ricoeur, Paul. Memory, History, Forgetting. Chicago: University of Chicago Press, 2004.

VI. Totalitarianism, Genocide, and Domination

Friedlander, Henry. The Origins of Nazi Genocide. Chapel Hill: University of North Carolina Press, 1995.

Burleigh, Michael. Death and Deliverance. Cambridge: Cambridge University Press, 1994.

Lifton, Robert Jay. The Nazi Doctors. New York: Basic Books, 1986.

Solzhenitsyn, Aleksandr. The Gulag Archipelago. New York: Harper & Row, 1974.

Applebaum, Anne. Gulag: A History. New York: Doubleday, 2003.

Akçam, Taner. A Shameful Act. New York: Metropolitan Books, 2006.

Suny, Ronald Grigor. They Can Live in the Desert but Nowhere Else. Princeton: Princeton University Press, 2015.

Human Rights Watch. Genocide in Iraq: The Anfal Campaign Against the Kurds. New Haven: Yale University Press, 1993.

Des Forges, Alison. Leave None to Tell the Story. New York: Human Rights Watch, 1999.

Straus, Scott. The Order of Genocide. Ithaca: Cornell University Press, 2006.

VII. Culture, Identity, Power, and Modernity

Taylor, Charles. A Secular Age. Cambridge, MA: Belknap Press, 2007.

MacIntyre, Alasdair. After Virtue. 3rd ed. Notre Dame, IN: University of Notre Dame Press, 2007.

Ellul, Jacques. Propaganda: The Formation of Men's Attitudes. New York: Vintage Books, 1973.

Berlin, Isaiah. Four Essays on Liberty. Oxford: Oxford University Press, 1969.

Nietzsche, Friedrich. On the Use and Abuse of History for Life. Indianapolis: Hackett, 1980.

VIII. Ritual, Tradition, and Sacred Time

Bradshaw, Paul F., and Maxwell E. Johnson. The Origins of Feasts, Fasts and Seasons in Early Christianity. Collegeville, MN: Liturgical Press, 2011.

Talley, Thomas J. The Origins of the Liturgical Year. 2nd ed. Collegeville, MN: Liturgical Press, 1991.

Hijmans, Steven. "Sol Invictus, the Winter Solstice, and the Origins of Christmas." Mouseion 3, no. 3 (2003): 377–398.

McGowan, Andrew. "How December 25 Became Christmas." Bible History Daily, December 2, 2016.

IX. Witness, Martyrdom, and Redemption

Foxe, John. Foxe's Book of Martyrs. Grand Rapids: Revell, 1981.

Nouwen, Henri J. M. The Wounded Healer. New York: Image Books, 1979.

Final Editorial Note

Appendix III exists not to overwhelm the reader, but to honor truth. Faith that cannot withstand examination is not faith, but fear. This work welcomes scrutiny — historical, philosophical, and theological — because truth does not retreat from light.

TABLE OF CONTENTS

The Paradox of Pain
Mariela G. George

APPENDICES

I now see…

It is for freedom that Christ has set us free. *Galatians 5:1*

www.ingramcontent.com/pod-product-compliance
Lightning Source LLC
LaVergne TN
LVHW010655110826
845149LV00014B/3104

* 9 7 9 8 9 9 3 4 5 8 8 6 1 *